mindfulness to go
How to **Meditate** While You're **On the Move**

WITHDRAWN

_____

David Harp, MA

New Harbinger Publications, Inc.

Publisher's Note

This publication is designed to provide accurate and authoritative information in regard to the subject matter covered. It is sold with the understanding that the publisher is not engaged in rendering psychological, financial, legal, or other professional services. If expert assistance or counseling is needed, the services of a competent professional should be sought.

Note 1: *If you are in a lot of physical or mental pain, it may be wise—and compassionate— to read this entire book before starting to work with the actual exercises. Just read about it, think about it (especially the sections on compassion and judging), but don't try to use the exercises until you really feel ready.*

Note 2: *If you have any physical impairments that restrict your motion, you will find that many of these exercises can be easily adapted for use by people in chairs. Comments or questions regarding this may be sent via the publisher to the author, who will attempt to address them.*

Distributed in Canada by Raincoast Books

Copyright © 2011 by David Harp
New Harbinger Publications, Inc.
5674 Shattuck Avenue
Oakland, CA 94609
www.newharbinger.com

Cover design by Amy Shoup; Text design by Michele Waters-Kermes; Acquired by Jess O'Brien; Edited by Clancy Drake

Library of Congress Cataloging-in-Publication Data

Harp, David.
  Mindfulness to go : how to meditate while you're on the move / David Harp.
    p. cm.
  Includes bibliographical references.
  ISBN 978-1-57224-989-9 (pbk.) -- ISBN 978-1-57224-990-5 (pdf e-book) 1.
Meditation. 2. Awareness. 3. Attention. I. Title.
  BF637.P36H37 2011
  158.1'2--dc22

                                    2011012530

13   12   11

10   9   8   7   6   5   4   3   2

Permissions

Some of the concepts contained in this book are also proprietary titles or main components of David's corporate presentations, including: Mental Muscle™, How to See It Coming, Before It Hits the Fan™, The Compassion Response™, and Mindfulness On the Fly™. Many of the compassion exercises and some of the other exercises are based on those in *The Three Minute Meditator* and *MetaPhysical Fitness,* and are used with the kind permission of David's co-author of those books, his twin sister, Dr. Nina Smiley.

Dedication to Elizabeth Kubler-Ross

I cannot really call her my teacher. But that one weekend workshop at the very beginning of my career helped me to make sense of the near-death, out-of-body experience that had led me to psychology in the first place.

My debt to her, and of course to my teachers Stephen and Ondrea Levine, and to Jack Kornfield (who put up with me on a weekly basis for far longer than anyone should have had to) is profound. Any credit that accrues from my work, in person or in writing, is a credit to these great teachers, but all misstatements, inaccuracies, and bad behavior on my part are entirely my own fault.

I'd also like to dedicate this book to the great physician and cardiologist Dr. Vincent De Quattro. His study of the role of stress and the sympathetic nervous system in disease was early and characteristically courageous, as was his commitment to following the facts as he saw them, wherever they led.

Contents

acknowledgments

My appreciation as always to my old friend and mentor Matthew McKay, Ph.D., for his help with this book as well as so many other things.

I'd also like to thank Joshua Boger and Justin Morreale. Joshua not just for his kindness to me and mine, but for the inspiration he provides by demonstrating that someone can be incredibly active and very kind and mindful as well. And Justin not just for his early and ongoing support of my work, but for the clarity of his own mindfulness that informs and infuses mindfulness in those with whom he comes in contact.

I must also acknowledge and thank three groups: the many tens of thousands of attendees at my corporate events, all of the students who have attended my longer workshops at the New York Open Center and the Kripalu Center, and my beloved children and wife, from whom I've learned so much.

introduction

Mindfulness used to seem like an unattainable dream to me. I had a vague understanding that the word referred to the ability to focus one's attention—somehow learning to pacify mental chatter—eventually leading (in theory, at least) to a more balanced, calm, and compassionate experience of life.

But my own mind and its constant thoughts—both pleasurable and frightening ones—seemed far beyond conscious control, and I was so busy, hectic, and stressed each day that I could not imagine finding the time to study and practice this crucial yet apparently inaccessible skill.

Now, after decades of practicing meditation and mindfulness, and years of training others—from hospice volunteers to CEOs—I know learning *what* mindfulness is takes only a few minutes of easy instruction, and that the basic exercises that produce it can be practiced *while* we do almost anything else that forms the fabric of our daily life. If you suffer from stress, from anger, from fear, from un-useful desires—as I always did—and don't believe you can find the time to improve the situation—as I always believed—then I've written this book for you.

I don't do it perfectly—almost no one does, except *maybe* the Dalai Lama—but the attempt has transformed my life, as it will yours if you try it. And in a very real sense, by practicing mindfulness on the go, you can learn to practice anytime, no matter what else you're doing, taking virtually no time at all.

Who Can Use This Book?

Perhaps you've heard and thought about mindfulness, or about developing the meditation practice that leads to it. Or perhaps the meaning of the term "mindfulness" is unclear to you, even if you understand, more or less, what a meditation exercise is. Maybe you've tried Transcendental Meditation, or one of many other meditation programs. But if you've never attempted a meditation or mindfulness practice, or if you've tried without much success, or did it "for a while" before abandoning it, please consider whether you've had the following thoughts, or variations on them:

- I just can't sit still long enough to meditate. I feel (or would feel) like jumping out of my skin.

- I don't have time to meditate.

- I tried, but I just couldn't concentrate (or couldn't imagine concentrating) on a mantra, or a sound, or a candle flame, or the feel of my breathing.

- Sit cross-legged for twenty minutes? Forget about it!

If you've had thoughts like these, it may be because you are a "bee" type of person. In chapter 1, I'll describe how I use animal labels (birds, bats, bees, and barnacles) to characterize various personality types and the meditation styles that are most likely to work for each type.

Unfortunately for those of us who are highly active, energetic, busy "bees," many of the most common forms of meditation are more appropriate for "barnacle" type folk. This means that these exercises are not likely to be either appealing or particularly well suited to your personal style when you're trying to develop a mindfulness practice. And that's why I wrote *this* book, outlining a mindfulness method created specifically for those of us who are just "too busy" or "too hyper" or "too active" to sit and meditate for half an hour. Naturally, "bird," "bat," or "barnacle" type people are more than welcome to use the method as well, if their lifestyle makes it difficult to find time to be mindful.

What's in the Book?

We'll begin, in chapter 1, with a look at what mindfulness is and isn't, examining the ways in which any action, physical or mental, can be either mindful or not mindful. Then with a single, simple experiment we'll experience how the application of mindfulness can instantly transform any physical action and any feeling. To say it another way, mindfulness transforms both motion and emotion.

Once you understand and experience the nature of mindfulness (however briefly), the rest of the book will provide concise but complete instructions on the types of exercises (also called meditations, or meditation exercises) that you can do no matter what else you're doing: there are driving meditations and walking meditations; talking meditations and meditations-while-listening; in-front-of-the-computer meditations; jogging meditations; shopping meditations; waiting-in-line meditations.

What do all these diverse-sounding exercises have in common? They are all designed to build what I call the "mental muscle" that allows us to develop and then maintain the state of mindfulness, no matter what's going on—or not going on. No matter what your typical day may be like, you'll find lots of ways to integrate these mindfulness-in-motion meditations into it. And you'll begin doing so—not just reading about it—almost immediately.

We'll end with a chapter on "self-soothing" meditations, in which we'll mindfully observe the ways in which we soothe ourselves when feeling needy or in pain—ways healthy and unhealthy, from singing in the shower to eating junk food in front of the TV. Observing these practices will allow us to emphasize the healthy ones and de-emphasize the less healthy ones. By the time you get to this part of the book, you'll have built up enough mental muscle, and experienced enough mindfulness practice built directly into your day, to do this in a compassionate, nonjudgmental, and effective way. Now it's time to get started!

mindfulness—
what, why, and how

Life is motion. From the orbits of the subatomic particles that provide the "stuff" of the universe to the migrations of species, movement is an intrinsic part of life. Yet many of us think that mindfulness—the transformative state of being that I'll describe in a moment—can be practiced only during a state of stillness, of sitting quietly in a bedroom or monastery. That's not just wrong, it's counterproductive—because we can both *learn* to be mindful, then *become* mindful…on the go. In fact, for many of us, learning to be mindful is actually easier when we do it while going about the movements of our regular daily life.

What Is Mindfulness?

There are many ways to define mindfulness. My own convenient, simple, and—most importantly—*useful* definition might be stated like this: the state of mind in which we can choose either to be fully aware on many different levels—whether physical, mental, or philosophical—at once, or to focus our awareness on any of these various levels at will.

Perhaps you feel as though you can already do this (stay aware of different levels of perception, or focus upon any of them at will). And perhaps you can. Walking down a quiet country road at night, you may find it easy to look up at the stars and marvel at the universe, then listen to the sound of your own footsteps in the road. Of course, driving down a congested street during rush hour with a car full of squabbling passengers and a gas gauge below empty may be a different story.

So, let's be honest with ourselves. Most of us, myself included (it's easier to preach than to practice), allow our minds and thoughts to have a great deal of control over our emotions, our words, and our actions.

Cultivating a state of mindfulness helps us to notice these un-useful thoughts, remember how to short-circuit the negative consequences they will produce if allowed to continue, and turn the focus of our attention back to the necessities of the situation. The exercises in this book will help you foster this state.

How Mindfulness Differs from Meditation

Mindfulness is the state we wish to achieve. Meditations are the exercises we do to get there. The relationship between the state of mindfulness and the meditation exercises that you'll begin practicing shortly is like the relationship between the state of being a great baseball player and the exercises of running, weight-training, batting practice, and catching practice.

What Is "Mental Muscle?"

"Mental muscle" is my own term for the ability to use the senses to direct the brain's attention to any particular object. Some objects, such as a James Bond movie, grab and hold our full attention with exciting chase scenes, beautiful faces and bodies, and villains with great lines. But staying focused on something that is *not* intrinsically interesting has certain costs to us. That's why our schoolteachers rarely asked us to "give" or "turn" our attention to lists of state capitals or times tables—they told us to "pay" attention to them.

Focusing on things that are easy to focus on, whether Hollywood movies or our own fears or angers, does not require mental muscle: the opposite is true. When we *lack* mental muscle, our attention naturally gravitates to those thoughts or things that are the most compelling or engrossing for us, even when this is not desirable. If you find yourself thinking about lunch when you're supposed to be working, or about work when you're supposed to be lunching, you could probably stand to build up your mental muscle.

It's *simple* to understand how to build physical muscle (barbell curls for biceps, crunches for abdominal muscles), but it's not *easy* to find the time or the will to practice the exercise over and over until you get the desired results. Just as physical muscle results from doing physical exercise, mental muscle results from doing meditative exercises. Simple, right? But again, not easy for many of us—especially for those of us who have never found a style or program of meditation that we can easily understand, and then stick to.

Birds, Bats, Barnacles, and Bees

In my earlier work, I developed the concept of "birds, bats, barnacles, and bees" in relation to meditation practice. These animal terms—simplistic though they may be—are an easy way to acknowledge the fact that most people have preferred modes of perceiving, processing, and using information. Birds have great eyesight: an eagle can spot a mouse from a mile up. People who are like "birds" in my terminology will tend to prefer visually-based meditation exercises, and they may prefer to learn meditation by a visual method: a person or DVD rather than a book or CD.

"Bats," as you may have guessed, are audio-preferring folk. They'll probably enjoy mantra (sound-based) meditations, and will want to learn by listening, not looking or feeling. "Barnacles" don't get around much, nor do they want to. They live in one place, and their tiny, feathery fingers constantly taste and test the water. Barnacle people like taste-and-smell meditations, or meditations that involve noticing physical sensation while one is not moving, such as focusing attention on the feeling of one's rear as it sits in a chair.

That brings us to the "bees." Bees—and I include myself in this category—are busy. Kinetic. In constant motion. You can guess what type of meditation exercises are most likely to be preferred by—and be most effective in fostering mindfulness for—us bees: meditations that produce a state of mindfulness… in motion.

Why We Need to Become More Mindful

There are lots of good reasons to understand and then cultivate a state of mindfulness. It is a many-leveled pursuit, not unlike learning a martial art. Some might begin a study of, say, tae kwon do with the goal of getting into slightly better shape. Others might begin with the intention of both getting into shape and becoming better able to defend themselves. A rare few might start tae kwon do practice with the ultimate goal of winning a medal at the Olympics, or of becoming so adept at the sport that it becomes a spiritual discipline in itself. Achieving these latter goals would naturally require a tremendous commitment of time and energy—and, most likely, a natural aptitude for the sport. Virtually anyone can learn to enjoy skiing or painting or tennis or boxing to some extent, but only a few are physically and mentally capable of becoming a Bode Miller, a Pablo Picasso, a Serena Williams, or a Muhammad Ali.

Similarly, it's possible to take a mindfulness practice to many levels. Not many will become fully enlightened gurus or saints. And that's fine, because integrating even small amounts of mindfulness practice into daily life can have an immediate and beneficial effect. How? In three words:

mindfulness reduces stress

So what? Well, in 2007, the American Psychological Association conducted a study called "Stress in America." Of 1,848 adults, 77 percent reported experiencing physical symptoms related to stress within the previous month and 73 percent of the participants reported experiencing psychological symptoms related to stress within the previous month. And that was before the recession hit.

If you've bothered to pick up this book and read even this far, you probably believe that a meditation-based mindfulness practice might very well improve your life. You don't need to aspire to guru status or sainthood (although you can if you like); you just want to reduce your stress level. But in the process, you're also likely to improve your:

- control of the emotions of anger and fear;

- interpersonal relationships;

- communication skills;

- ability to handle unhealthy desires, whether they involve sex, food, or watching junk online or on TV;

- issues with any kind of performance anxiety, from golf to test-taking.

With practice and patience, you'll increase your level of self-awareness. You'll be calmer overall and more responsive to any situation. If you have a religious or spiritual orientation, you may choose to deepen your pursuit of mindfulness to enhance your sense of connectedness to what some call "God," and others call "spiritual consciousness" or "the underlying ground of being." But (perhaps most importantly for most of us) simply knowing what mindfulness is and having some practice in achieving it will give us a tool that we can use anywhere, anytime, to put ourselves in charge of our own lives.

Summing Up

- Mindfulness is the state in which we can choose to be fully aware of many different levels of perception at once. There are many levels of mindfulness, but even the most basic will give you immediate benefits by reducing stress.

- When we are in the mindful state, we have increased control over what we are paying attention to. We are controlling our minds, not vice versa.

- Meditations are mental exercises that build "mental muscle." Mental muscle is what allows us to have the power and discipline to choose where our attention goes.

2

motion, emotion, and the fight-or-flight response

When I'm simply walking down the street, it's difficult for the casual observer to determine my mental state (unless, for example, I'm running erratically while pulling at my hair). I may be thinking about where I'm going and what I'm going to do when I get there, or about some past insult or indignity, real or imagined. Or my mental attention may be focused on the physical sensation of walking, or on the number of steps I take during each inhale and each exhale as I breathe. No one can tell, and that's a good thing. Because it means that you or I can discreetly practice building the mental muscle that leads to mindfulness even as we amble down the road.

Mindful Motion versus Nonmindful Motion

Even though no one else can see it, there is a big, big difference between mindful motion and nonmindful motion. For example, while walking mindfully we can pay attention to and be aware of a variety of different sensations, thoughts, emotions, and philosophical issues, either one at a time or all at the same time, such as:

- the physical sensation of our feet landing on the ground as we walk;

- the appearance and disappearance (as we notice them and swiftly remove our attention from them) of any non-walking-related thoughts;

- our level of emotional attachment to the destination we approach;

- the historical, psychological, and philosophical reasons we are heading there in the first place.

During nonmindful motion, our natural tendency is to give to our motion only the parts of our brain necessary for locomotion—to move on autopilot. The rest of that magnificent organ is often engaged in completely non-motion-related activity, such as generating and then focusing on emotions like fears and angers, and on other mental constructions such as plans for the future, memories of the past, and judgments on anything that appears before us in real life or in our minds.

What Are "Emotions" and the "Fight-or-Flight Response"?

Certain of these mental activities (such as fears and angers) are, like the act of locomotion itself, likely to be on autopilot, in a certain sense. That is, they are likely to be unexamined, and thus uncontrolled. Emotions are often the result of a natural process in the brain known as the "fight-or-flight response."

This particular brain function began to evolve many hundreds of millions of years ago, and was essential in allowing our ancestors to survive. When the minnow sees the shadow of a larger fish, its tiny brain produces a hard-wired flight response, and it darts into the sheltering weeds. When the male crocodile sees another male encroaching on its territory, its fight response is triggered, and it attacks.

This same ancient fight-or-flight response process remains in our own rather larger brains, so that when the taxi appears to be heading straight toward us, we flee to safety without a second's thought, as our flight response kicks in. If the threat is not amenable to flight—an attack by a dog, for example—we'll probably grab any potential weapon at hand and do our best to fight. Not only are the flight response and the fight response useful in situations like these, they are reflexive and almost unavoidable.

Since the purpose of the fight-or-flight response is to save the life of the organism, it has a very powerful effect on the body. During the response, your body is suffused with glandular secretions (like adrenaline), and the result is that:

- digestion stops, so that all available energy can be sent to the muscular system in order for you to run or do battle;

- blood leaves the extremities to pool in the center of the body, so that you don't bleed to death as quickly if you get bitten or scratched (this raises your blood pressure);

- as extra energy reaches the musculoskeletal system, you have greater strength (but it also puts more stress on bones, tendons, and muscles).

The Downside of the Fight-or-Flight Response

Although potentially lifesaving, the effects listed above also cause physiological stresses. If these reactions were to take place only when you need to avoid saber-toothed tigers, rabid dogs, or out-of-control taxis, the stresses—interrupted digestion, heightened blood pressure, and taxed musculoskeletal system—would be well worth the escape from disaster. But as it turns out, our big, complex brains complicate the matter, with the mental "objects" commonly known as "thoughts."

The Power of Thought

Imagine, right now, your favorite type of car, or a childhood pet. You've created a thought that is a brain-generated picture, or "visualization," of that object. You can mentally "see" its color, its shape, its size in relation to your own. Perhaps you can imagine what it would feel like to put your hand on the car's fender or stroke the pet's fur. This image has a certain reality, even though it does not exist outside your head.

Regrettably, the fight-or-flight response reacts to a mental image in much the same way as it would to an actual, real-life threat. If you imagine that your boss is approaching you with a pink slip in hand, your fight-or-flight response will kick in with almost as much ferocity as it would had the actual event occurred.

Thus many of us have a dozen—or a hundred—fight-or-flight responses every day, triggered by nothing more real than pictures in our minds. In light of the physiological side effects of the fight-or-flight response, it's no surprise that we may suffer from excessive indigestion, high blood pressure, and pain.

Different Degrees of the Fight-or-Flight Response

Now, having a fight-or-flight response doesn't mean that you immediately start throwing punches or running like the wind. Rather, it means that your brain has told your body to get ready to do one or both of those things. This preparation might proceed to actual fighting or fleeing, or it could be short-circuited either immediately or eventually.

For example, the boss's dirty look or harsh criticism could prompt in us a fight-or-flight response that involves—according to our nature—getting into a shouting match with him or running away to hyperventilate in a bathroom stall. Or we might quash our fighting or fleeing behavior, silently enduring the encounter while still experiencing the internal stresses of raised blood pressure, roiled digestion, and knotted neck and shoulder muscles. If we choose to develop some mental muscle, however, we can then defuse our fight-or-flight response not only before we take any action, but before any of these significant physiological symptoms occur.

The Difference Between Fight and Flight

The difference between a "fight" response and a "flight" response can be understood as the difference between anger and fear. Many of us show a preference for, or tendency toward, one response over the other. When speaking of these preferences, I often refer to people as being "grizzlies" (tending toward anger and the fight response) or "gazelles" (who would rather flee than fight). Those who tend to freeze when they feel threatened I call "possums," since that creature will play dead when threatened. Some of us (including me) may respond in more than one way.

Fight responses produce tightening symptoms in the body—fists and teeth clench as though to hit and bite. Flight responses produce what I call "loosey-goosey symptoms"—proverbial butterflies in the stomach, a tingling in the scalp, shuddering, and flinching. I like to refer to the somatic (bodily) effects of the fight-or-flight response as "symptoms," because when they're not needed to protect life and limb, these effects are like the symptoms of a disease. The name of that "disease" is the "stress response."

The Stress Response

If stress is such a common phenomenon—especially in our age and culture—it must have some kind of positive purpose, right? Wrong. Fight-or-flight responses certainly can serve a useful purpose, but stress, as I define it, does not.

In my own definition, "useful" fight-or-flight responses are simply appropriate—and temporary—reactions to dangerous real-life situations. When the situation is over, the body (and brain) return to normal. No more danger? No more fight-or-flight response.

I define "stress" as the result of an extended series of *unuseful* fight-or-flight responses triggered by repetitive thoughts. When we're involved in a difficult situation, we may think of it dozens of times a day, each time producing a fight-or-flight response. And each of these individual responses triggers the symptoms that interrupt your digestion, raise your blood pressure, and strain your musculoskeletal system. If you have many in a row, day after day, the pernicious effects of each one of them run into the effects of the next, producing a virtually continuous fight-or-flight response: that is, a stress response.

As though these immediately negative symptoms of stress were not enough, stress is also believed to increase the risk, intensity, or likelihood of: headache; abuse of drugs, alcohol, and tobacco; depression; impaired sleep; neck and back pain; fatigue; cardiovascular disease; asthma; and possibly even cancer.

Short-Circuiting the Stress Response

Long before human beings (with our unique ability to produce mental images within the brain) existed, our more primitive ancestors had a great way to reverse the fight-or-flight response. As soon as the crisis situation that caused the fight-or-flight response was no longer a danger—once that minnow had reached the weeds, or that crocodile had vanquished his opponent—an equal but opposite response would kick in. This "relaxation response," as it is sometimes called, reverses the physiological changes brought on by the fight-or-flight response. Digestion resumes, blood pressure returns to normal, and muscles relax, taking the tension off of the bones and tendons. Thus neither the grizzly nor the gazelle nor the possum must live in a constant state of stressful arousal. When they need it, it's there. When they don't, it's not.

For us, with our repetitive stress-inducing thoughts, it's not so simple. But we can find a way to get back to a proper balance between stressful arousal and normal-state relaxation. It all starts with our breathing.

The Power of the Breath

Everyone knows that breathing is important—we can't last for long without it. However, you may not yet know that focusing your mental attention on the process of breathing is the fastest and easiest way to short-circuit a stress response.

Once again, the concept is simple, but it's not always easy to implement. Especially when we are frightened or angry, it's easy to forget that these un-useful (or, as mindfulness practitioners and teachers often prefer to say, "unskillful") stress responses have such a simple solution.

Summing Up

- When in motion—whether walking, jogging, or driving—we can be either mindful or not mindful. No one else can tell, which makes it easier to practice mindfulness on the go.

- The ancient fight-or-flight response was originally designed to preserve a creature's life. It would kick in when it was needed in a crisis, then the animal would revert to its normal state.

- The fight-or-flight response stops your digestive process, raises your blood pressure, and stresses your musculoskeletal system.

- The fight-or-flight response is useful when you are being attacked, or when you are stuck under a cement mixer.

- When it occurs dozens of times a day in response to nothing more real than thoughts, the fight-or-flight response is un-useful, and even harmful, causing all kinds of other physical and mental problems.

- Luckily for us, un-useful fight-or-flight responses can be short-circuited simply by focusing our mental attention on the process of breathing. And that's what we're going to start doing, right away.

3

meditation in motion: the most basic mental muscle exercises

Enough talking. Enough history. Enough theory. It's time for you to demonstrate for yourself, in a simple and preliminary way, both the potential benefits of a mindfulness practice and the ways in which meditation exercises can lead to this state. All you'll need to do the experiment is a moment of your time, your feet, and the mental muscle to force yourself to perform such a seemingly inconsequential set of actions. Please bear with me. This one is so simple that it may seem trivial, or even too simple to try. But that does not mean it isn't important to do it, and to the best of your ability.

Exercise 1: Walking and Counting Meditation

1. Stand up. Mentally prepare to count each step you take; you'll be counting each one every time your foot hits the floor.

2. Walk around the room at a medium-slow pace. If you are outside or in a very large room, just walk in a circle that will take you ten or twenty seconds to circumnavigate.

3. As you walk, mentally count the number of steps that it takes you to complete the task. Make sure that you count every step—it's important.

4. Sit back down.

If you had trouble keeping an accurate count (which most of you won't), try again until it seems easy.

Please note that many of the following exercises will involve mentally counting, and later on labeling, physical actions such as taking steps or breaths. To avoid redundancy, I won't include the "preparation" as a part of the exercise directions from now on, so please be sure to read all of the numbered elements of each exercise before you begin.

Now, let's add another step to the very beginning of the exercise, this time using a thought that generally produces *minor* annoyance or *slight* anxiety when it comes into your mind. This should not be a thought that's likely to result in raging anger, nor should it be your deepest fear. But when you think of it, you should be able to notice at least slight symptoms of a fight response (tightening fists, clenching teeth) or a flight response (stomach butterflies, tingling scalp).

Now repeat exercise 1, with this added first step:

Exercise 2: Walking and Counting Meditation with Negative Thought

1. Bring the mildly negative thought into your mind. Stay with it until you notice any symptoms of fight (anger) or flight (fear) response.

2. Stand up.

3. Walk around the room.

4. As you walk, count the number of steps it takes you to complete your walk. Make sure that you do this with *great accuracy*.

5. Sit back down.

Now think about what you just did, and how it felt. You will most likely find that as your mental attention shifted from a focus on the annoying thought to the walking meditation, the thought stopped having any effect on you: it may, in fact, have disappeared. I often do this exercise with groups, ranging from kindergarteners to CEOs to hospice patients. After they've done the simple meditation, I always ask, "What happened to the annoying thought?" Perhaps the most succinct yet comprehensive answer I've ever gotten to this question came from a six-year-old. "Poof," he said. Meaning, "It just disappeared." And I imagined a fragile soap bubble bursting, with no residue, and barely a sound.

Now What?

You've gotten the first, most basic, and most important lesson under your belt: that if you can remove your mental attention from a thought, that thought loses any power to affect you.

For most of us, switching the focus of our mental attention from the annoying thought to the careful physical perception of the number of steps in our little walk is enough to short-circuit a mild fight-or-flight response. We've *chosen* to pay attention to a different level of perception: we're focusing on physical action instead of thought. And this is the first stage of mindfulness: beginning to learn to choose when and where to focus our mental attention. For now, exploring the act of purposeful mental focus on events that are not intrinsically interesting (like counting the number of our footsteps) is our only task.

The extremely simple exercises in this chapter will prepare you for the more complicated—and more powerful—exercises that follow. You don't need to spend lots of time with these unless you want to, and you can probably do all of the exercises in this chapter in one session of ten or fifteen minutes, including the reading. For now, you're just exploring.

Your job, over the course of the next few chapters, will be to try lots of different meditation exercises and decide which seem best to fit your day-to-day activities. This exploration and practice will also start to build the mental muscle that will help you more easily reach a state of mindfulness.

If This Seems Dumb, or Boring

It's too bad that the pursuit of mindfulness can't be fun and entertaining. But building mental muscle requires intense focus on things that are just not intrinsically interesting—it requires willing your mind to stay on the object that you've chosen. Just like you've got to keep on doing boring, repetitive, painful barbell curls if you want big biceps. If you're bored, you might try walking faster, or even jogging or running, as you practice these exercises. But that's as far in the direction of entertainment as I'd recommend you go. It's work: it's not always fun, but it's always worth the effort.

More Very Simple Walking Meditation Exercises

In this next exercise, instead of counting each step, you will simply "label" it with a word. Again, no matter how foolish or simplistic the exercise may seem, do it to the best of your ability. It won't take long.

Exercise 3: Walking and Labeling Meditation

1. Stand up.

2. Walk around the room, mentally saying "step" each time your foot hits the floor.

3. Make sure that you do this with *great care*, without missing a single step—it's important.

4. Sit back down.

Since this exercise does not require you to keep track of changing numbers while you walk, you may find that thoughts are more likely to arise while you're doing it. If so, that's fine. That's a good piece of information to have: that, for you, thoughts are more likely to arise unbidden during labeling meditations than during counting meditations. At least for now. Whether or not this is the case for you, try this next variation on the walking and counting exercise.

Exercise 4: Walking and Counting Meditation

1. Stand up.

2. Walk around the room at a medium-slow, steady pace and, as you walk, count your steps until you get to four. Then start again with one, count to four, start again, and so on.

3. Sit back down.

Did that seem easier or harder than counting the total number of steps you took? Was it easier or harder to stay focused on this than on the step-labeling exercise? (If you've been a musician or in the military, this exercise may actually be *too* easy—without more practice, it may allow thoughts other than counting to enter your mind.)

Meditation and the Breath

Now it's time to switch our focus to the breath. It's a bit more subtle of an object than steps are, but the following exercise should still be relatively easy, even though it is a very effective meditation technique. If you did nothing but this exercise every single time you walked anywhere for the rest of your life, it would have profound and long-lasting benefits.

Exercise 5: Walking and Breath-Labeling Meditation

1. Stand up, and exhale comfortably and completely.

2. As you begin to inhale, begin walking around the room at a medium-slow pace. Just breathe normally—whatever that is for you, when walking. As you walk, you will provide a mental label for each inhale and each exhale.

3. Mentally say "in" for as long as the inhale lasts: "iiiiiiiiinnnn."

4. As you switch to the exhale, mentally say "out" for as long as the exhale lasts: "oooooouuuuuttt."

5. Do this until you've labeled at least three complete breaths (both inhale and exhale). (You may need to do a few laps, depending on how quickly you tend to breathe while walking.)

6. Sit down again.

Reflect on the exercise. Was it easy to stay with the labeling? Did thoughts intrude? Was this harder for you to stay focused on than the other walking exercises? Or was it easier, or about the same? You don't need to judge yourself ("I'm no good at this") or me ("This book is too simple"). Just investigate. Just observe. And when you're ready, go on to chapter 4.

Summing Up

- Try the exercises in this chapter. Investigate which seem easier to stay focused on, and which seem harder. That's really your only job for right now.

- The exercises may seem overly simplistic, or dumb, or boring. That's okay. Making your mind stay with something that it does not really want to do is what builds mental muscle.

- By the time you got to exercise 5, you were (for a few seconds, at least) using a technique that even advanced meditators find effective.

4

more mental muscle
exercises: variations
on the basics

Chapter 3 began with a demonstration of a crucial if perhaps obvious-seeming point: that removing mental attention from a thought that was triggering a stress response short-circuited the effects of that stress response. (Remember, please, that we are now categorizing all non-essential-for-self-preservation fight-or-flight responses as "stress responses," since that is all they are good for!)

In that chapter you began to practice meditations incorporating the techniques of counting, labeling, and breathing, all while your body was in motion (walking). After each exercise, you reflected on how easy or difficult it had been for you to focus your attention during the exercise.

Steps on the Path

Before we add to our repertoire of meditation exercises, let's think about why we're doing this. If you are reading these words, you probably want to integrate a degree of mindfulness into your life. This worthy but ambitious goal will require the mastery of a number of preliminary steps. The first of these—understanding what mindfulness is, and learning how the fight-or-flight response affects our bodies and how we can short-circuit this stress response—can be acquired simply by reading about them, which you've already done. The next steps require that you learn some basic meditation exercises. You've done some of that already, and in this chapter you'll do more.

Beginning musicians learn scales and practice playing single notes with the best tone possible. Beginning basketball players practice dribbling and passing. These skills alone won't get them to Carnegie Hall or Madison Square Garden, but without them, our would-be musicians and athletes will get nowhere at all.

Mindfulness Requires Reducing Fear, Anger, and Stress

In order to expand our capacity for mindfulness, we must learn to overcome the obstacles of fear and anger, lessening the stress they produce in our lives. When fear, anger, and stress dominate our attention, we can't be mindful. And loosening the grip these emotional states have on us requires that we build enough mental muscle to short-circuit our stress responses as they happen.

Turning one's mental attention to the breathing process is an excellent way to reverse the stress response; therefore, breath-based meditation exercises are among the most important things we need to practice. However, those of us who are kinetic, busy, "bee" folk are likely to find it difficult to focus on "just the breath" for very much time at all. This is neither good nor bad—it's just useful information to have. It simply means we'll need to add some motion to our meditation. Stay with me for a bit more instruction and one more stationary breathing meditation, and then we'll, quite literally, get moving.

Beginning to Breathe

Your first exercise based on the breath was exercise 5, in the previous chapter. This meditation technique, which is from the Tibetan Vipassana tradition, involves nothing more complex than labeling each inhale and exhale with the words "in" and "out" as you are performing that part of each breath.

Some of you may know that in addition to writing and speaking on cognitive science and mindfulness, I also write about, speak about, and play blues harmonica. We blues harp players must be very aware of our breathing, since inhaling or exhaling affects the notes we're playing. If you don't play harmonica, you may not be quite so attentive to your breath.

So please spend just a moment now observing your internal workings as you breathe. The plate-shaped muscle known as the diaphragm stretches across your chest cavity below the lungs. When you inhale, you start with your lungs relatively empty. Your diaphragm flexes downward, forcing the lungs to expand and fill with air. When you exhale, the diaphragm flexes upward to force air out of the lungs through the mouth and nose.

Place your hands over the upper part of your belly to feel this expansion/contraction process in your own body as you take a few breaths. Now you're ready for a new meditation.

Exercise 6: Seated Meditation with Breath-Labeling and Counting

1. Sit in a comfortable position. When you feel ready, you will begin the next step at the end of a comfortably complete exhale.

2. As you begin to inhale, mentally label this part of the breath with the words "iiiinnn...one." Try to time the

two words so that you finish just about when you are ready to begin exhaling.

3. As you switch from the inhale to the exhale, begin to label the exhale with the words "ouuuttt...one." Again, try to time the words so that you are finished just before your lungs are completely (but not uncomfortably) empty.

4. As you begin the inhale of the next breath, repeat step 2, but with a new number: "iiiinnn...two."

5. As you begin the exhale of that breath, repeat step 3, with a new number: "ouuuttt...two."

6. Do this for two more breaths: "iiiinnn...three, ouuuttt... three" and "iiiinnn...four, ouuuttt...four."

7. Stop. And think, for just a moment, whether that was easier, or more difficult, in comparison to exercises 1 through 5.

Staying Focused: What's Easy for You? What's Hard?

As I've said before, it's easy to keep our attention focused on an exciting crime novel or hilarious TV comedy. But it's the act of keeping one's attention focused on something that is not intrinsically interesting that builds mental muscle. Thus the beginning practitioner of meditation has a problem. The more subtle and elusive the object of meditation, the more mental muscle the student will build from staying focused on it. But if it's too hard to hold on to, the student is likely to just quit (as I did so many times in my early attempts at meditation). So finding the meditation exercises that work for us involves trying many different ones, and finding a balance between the subtlety of the object of the meditation and how easy it is to stay focused on it. James Bond movies provide too easy a focus for most of us, while attempting a deep mental focus on the mystery of the absolute is probably too hard.

When I use the terms "easy" and "hard," I am not attaching any judgment to them, and hope that you don't either. For many if not most of us, judgment—whether of ourselves or of others— is a category of thought that produces psychological pain and stress. In a later chapter, we'll discuss ways to deal with judging thoughts when they arise. But for now, please try not to judge your ability to do the exercises: just notice which ones are easier to complete, and which ones are more difficult to stay focused on. This is all simply useful information.

Since exercise 6, above, combines both counting and labeling, many people will find that performing it successfully (that is, keeping the count accurate while trying to match your two-word phrase to the length of each inhale and exhale) is easier than doing just the labeling, as in exercise 5. Having to keep mental track of two processes (labeling and counting) at the same time is somewhat hard; thus it helps us to maintain a relatively strong mental focus on the meditation.

But we are bees. We like to be busy. So it's time, now that you've had a chance to try this exercise while seated, to do it while on the go—at least insofar as walking around the room is "on the go."

Exercise 7: Walking Meditation with Breath-Labeling and Counting

1. Stand up. You will begin the next step at the end of a comfortably complete exhale.

2. As you begin to inhale, begin walking at a slow, steady, and comfortable pace. Mentally label your inhale with the words "iiiinnn...one." Try to time the two words so that you finish just as you're ready to exhale.

3. As you begin to exhale, label this part of the breath with the words "ouuuttt...one." Again, try to time the words so that you are finished just before your lungs are completely (but not uncomfortably) empty.

4. As you begin the inhale of the next breath, repeat step 2, but with a new number: "iiiinnn...two."

5. As you begin the exhale of that breath, repeat step 3 with a new number: "ouuuttt...two."

6. Do this for two more breaths: "iiiinnn...three, ouuuttt... three" and "iiiinnn...four, ouuuttt...four."

7. Stop. Reflect. Easy? Hard? No judging, just observing.

Beginning to Customize Your Meditation Practice

Did it feel easier or harder to stay focused during this moving meditation than it felt during the seated breathing meditation (exercise 6)? You're the only person who can tell how something feels to you. So as you continue to explore the meditation exercises in this chapter, try to notice how difficult it feels to keep your focus on each task. This will help you when you get to chapter 5, which is about customizing your mindfulness method.

As you experiment, ask yourself: Does labeling keep you focused better than counting? Or is the reverse true? Does doing both simultaneously help you stay focused? Does doing both at the same time make it too difficult to focus? Is it easier for you to focus on the breath when sitting, or when walking?

Exercise 8: Longer Walking Meditation with Breath-Labeling and Counting

This exercise is just like the last one, but longer. You'll simply keep on walking until you've labeled and counted ten breaths instead of four. You may need to double back or walk in circles to finish the exercise, depending on the space you're in. That's fine: just keep walking, breathing, labeling, and counting.

As in exercise 7, try to time the words so that you are finished saying them to yourself just before you're completely (but not uncomfortably) ready to change the direction of your breath.

If you are unable to get to ten without losing count, see if the following exercise is easier for you to stay focused on. There is no self-criticism, no judging; you're just learning what works best for you.

Exercise 9: Longer Walking Meditation with Breath-Labeling and Counting

For this exercise, you will do exercise 7 (in which you both labeled and counted your breaths until you reached four complete breaths), and immediately repeat it. This will give you a total of eight complete breaths; as before, you may need to double back or walk in circles to finish the exercise. Ask yourself: Was I able to keep my count in both exercises, or not? Was it easier to do exercise 8 (ten breaths) or exercise 9 (two sets of four breaths each)?

How Many Exercises Should I Do? And Where?

For now, your objective is just to try a number of different meditation exercises, then evaluate how easy or difficult it was to stay focused on each task. Once you've begun to customize a mindfulness program, you'll do multiple repetitions of your chosen meditations. Right now, go wide rather than deep: try all of the chapter 3 and 4 exercises once or twice, or at most three times. Experiment with doing these meditations in a slightly different place than you used before—sit in a different chair; walk in a different room. Eventually, you'll want to feel comfortable and ready to do these exercises wherever you are; it's a good idea to start building that flexibility now.

Adding a Step

In the following two exercises, you will stop counting breaths and return to counting steps. But you will still stay focused on your breathing. How does that work? You'll go for a little walk, and begin to count the number of steps you take during each inhale and each exhale. This may feel complicated at first, but many active people find this to be one of their favorite mental-muscle builders. In the next exercise, you will only count the steps you take during the exhalation. The exercise is designed to help you figure out how many steps you can comfortably take during a single exhalation—and thus, during a single complete breath, which you'll do in exercise 11.

Exercise 10: Walking Meditation with Step-Counting on the Exhale

1. Stand up. You will begin the next meditation at the end of a comfortably complete inhale.

2. Exactly as you start to exhale, take your first step (labeling it "one") and continue walking at a slow, steady, and comfortable pace.

3. As you continue to exhale, label each step with a number, saying (or whispering, or thinking) the number of the step as your foot hits the floor. Breathe comfortably. Don't try for a high count. Don't try for a low count. Just observe how many steps it's comfortable to take during each exhale.

4. When you start to feel empty, breathe in and, as you inhale, stop counting your steps.

5. Continue for half a dozen exhales' worth of walking and counting.

After this exercise, ask yourself: Did I have a similar number of steps during each exhale? Or did my counts vary a lot?

For most people, the number of steps taken during exhales tends to be roughly the same from breath to breath, perhaps varying by one or at most two steps. Naturally, if you speed up or slow down as you walk, your number of steps per exhale will reflect this. So try to keep your speed and walking conditions consistent when doing this exercise—at least for now. And remember, you're not going for high or low counts, just observing what is happening.

Once you've determined your average step count per exhale, you're ready for the next exercise.

Exercise 11: **Walking Meditation with Breath-Labeling and Step-Counting**

In this meditation, you will choose an average number of steps to take during each exhale *and* each inhale. For example, if the last exercise showed that you tend to take three steps during each exhale, you will coordinate your walking and your breathing so that you take three steps during each exhale and three steps during each inhale. If four steps was your average in the last exercise, you'll do the same, but with four steps during each inhale and four steps during each exhale. In the following description, I'll use three steps as my average; your number may be different, and that's fine.

1. Stand up. Inhale comfortably and completely. Be ready to start walking as you begin your exhale.

2. Begin your exhale just as your foot hits the floor for your first step.

3. As you exhale and step, mentally label the first step with the word "out," exactly as your foot hits the floor. Label the next steps of your exhale as "two" and "three," so that you are labeling the entire sequence as "out...two...three" (or "out...two...three...four" if you're exhaling over four steps, and so on).

4. When your lungs are comfortably empty, begin your inhale just as your foot hits the floor, and do the same

labeling and counting, with each label word coming exactly as each foot hits the floor: "in...two...three."

5. Continue this for at least four complete breaths. If you like, do it for longer.

Control the intensity of your breathing so that you exhale to a comfortable extent during the three steps (or however many steps you found were comfortable during exercise 10), and inhale to a comfortable extent during the next three steps. If you feel as though your lungs are getting too empty or too full, try decreasing the number of steps, using two steps instead of three, for example. If you feel as though you are forcing yourself to breathe more force-fully than you normally would, try increasing the number of steps, using four steps instead of three, for example.

This is probably my single favorite mental muscle exercise, and the easiest to integrate into my daily life. I'll tell you how to do that for yourself in the next chapter.

Summing Up

- In order to become mindful, we need to reduce the hold that anger, fear, and stress so often have on us.

- Reducing the grip of stressful emotions can be achieved by building up sufficient mental muscle to turn the attention to the breathing process, no matter what mental or physical condition or situation we are in.

- To build that mental muscle, we must try to keep our attention focused on one or more meditation exercises. And we need to apply our attention to exercises with a breath focus.

- By trying a number of different meditation techniques and analyzing how hard or easy it is to stay focused, you'll soon be able to customize your mindfulness development program. So make sure you've tried all of the exercises in chapters 3 and 4 at least once.

- People who are bees—kinetic, active, busy—are most likely to find it easier to stay focused while in motion.

- As you try the exercises, just notice which techniques are easier for you to focus on, and which are harder. Don't judge—just notice.

5

customizing your mindfulness method

In chapter 4 you tried (I hope) a variety of meditation exercises of increasing sophistication, ending with the incredibly useful and important exercise 11, which combines breathing with labeling and step-counting.

In many spiritual and meditative traditions, there's a story that goes something like this. The great sage goes to an island where the residents, although very spiritually oriented, know only one spiritual practice. Throughout their waking life, whenever their attention is not on some useful physical or interpersonal task, they count their breaths up to three. They do it a lot. But they never get up to four, and they never do anything else.

The great sage, of course, knows a great many meditations, and has lengthy metaphysical explanations for why each one is important. After a full month (or year, or decade) the sage departs, his work finished, the natives now educated to his satisfaction. As his ship is carrying him back to the mainland, he notices a blur above the water behind him, rapidly approaching. It is the entire population of the island, running across the surface of the water! "O Great One," they cry. "We have already forgotten your instructions." And the sage, properly chastened, recognizes the power of a simple practice, diligently followed.

The lesson of the islanders is that for most of us, diligence will trump diversity and depth when it comes to the benefits of a mindfulness practice. Using a few simple meditations—or even one—that we can integrate into our daily life and use when needed will help us more than knowing lots of advanced mindfulness theory or many dozens of complex exercises. Eventually, after you've used simple techniques to begin to clear your mind of fear, anger, un-useful desire, and stress, you may want to study those more esoteric things. But for now, we'll take the islanders' example as our model, and learn to customize a few simple, easy-to-implement mindfulness practices that will help us to build mental muscle, starting right now.

Which Meditation Should You Start With?

You should start with the easiest meditation—the easiest one for you, that is. Which of the exercises in chapters 3 and 4 were easier for you to stay focused on, and which were harder? A very basic way of determining your level of focus during a meditation exercise involving counting is this: were you able to keep an accurate count? For meditations involving labeling, assess your focus by asking yourself, "Did I notice that I was thinking about something entirely different and had completely forgotten to label my steps?"

For you, was counting and labeling breaths (as in exercise 7) easier than just labeling them (as in exercise 5), or harder? Was exercise 7, in which it was breaths that you labeled and counted, easier or harder, focus-wise, than the one in which you labeled and counted steps (exercise 11)? Don't obsess over this, but do think about it for a moment, especially if one (or more) exercises were significantly easier or more difficult for you to stay focused on.

"Easy" versus "Hard": Which Is Better?

Is "easy" or "hard" better? It depends. When you're a near or total beginner, doing meditation exercises that are easy enough to stay focused on for at least the better part of a minute (long enough, say, to label and count four breaths) is good. But once you can do that with some reliability, it's time to do something just a bit more challenging. If you were not in great shape when embarking on a physical exercise program, you might start doing pushups with your knees on the ground. But once you'd gained some strength, a good instructor would help you segue into regular pushups.

What might a "harder" meditation be like? Well, it's harder to stay focused for a longer time than a shorter one, so you might want to experiment with counting and labeling up to ten breaths, or twenty, or more (when I started, ten was quite a challenge). Some of the meditations in later parts of this book may also be more difficult for you. However, if you need more of a focus challenge, simply doing longer versions of the exercises you've already tried will be fine for now.

Maintaining Reasonable Expectations

The last thing you need from a program that's supposed to decrease your mental stress is a new set of "shoulds." Your goal is to observe and explore, not self-criticize. That said, there is a certain bottom line to this process: as soon as you can, you will need to be able to stay focused for at least four breaths' worth of time on either exercise 7 or exercise 11.

If you cannot yet do this with either exercise, you have four choices.

1. Keep on reading while you practice trying to do those two exercises. As you read, I recommend returning to whichever one seems easier at least

once every few pages until you can reliably stay focused for four breaths' worth of time.

2. Keep reading and see if one of the breath-based exercises later in this chapter seems easier for you to stay focused on.

3. Take a break from reading and just work on either exercise 7 or exercise 11 until you can reliably stay focused for four breaths' worth of time.

4. Should these exercises still seem really hard for you, try this. If you can stay focused for even one single breath's worth of exercise 7 ("iiiinnnn...one, ouutttt...one") before you lose count, or just one single breath's worth of exercise 11 ("in...two... three, out...two...three"), that's fine—as long as you follow the "Important Instructions for When You Lose It," which precede exercise 13, below. Please read those instructions right now, if you fall into this category.

Walking Meditations: When, Where, and How Long

In many of my instructions, I'll ask you to do a particular exercise that involves walking for "a moment" or "half a minute or so." These are approximations, since my main interest is in frequency rather than in duration. I want you to do lots of these meditations every day, for only as long as seems convenient to you.

So, when should you meditate, where, and for how long? Simple: anytime and anywhere. Mindfulness on the go is the polar opposite of meditation approaches that suggest you spend long periods of concentrated meditation in some isolated location. Certainly, doing that can build up mental muscle quickly. I attend retreats occasionally, and I do feel incredibly energized and rejuvenated after a five- or ten-day meditation retreat, and my mindfulness level is about as high as it's likely to get. However, if I don't continue my day-to-day, minute-by-minute, integrated meditation practice, the benefits of the retreat soon diminish.

Identifying Situational Opportunities

Now's the time to identify a few situations in your life into which you can insert a short meditation exercise. Think of times at which you have to walk from one place to another—not necessarily a long walk, since you'll be doing an exercise that's only four breaths long. Many of my students find that walking from their computer to the water cooler or a shared printer or the bathroom at work is a perfect time to do a short walking and breathing exercise.

My office is on the second floor, and everything and everyone else is on the first. I climb those stairs thirty or forty times a day, and on the wall near the stairs I have a sign: "Mind the stairs." It's there to remind me to be mindful *every single time* I go up or down. As my foot hits the first of the stairs, I note whether I'm inhaling or exhaling, and instantly go into a walking meditation with breath-labeling and step-counting (like exercise 11). When I reach the end of the fourteen stairs, I either stop, or continue the exercise as I continue to walk.

Your Daily Commitment: At Least Six Times Each Day

I'd like you to identify at least six opportunities to do a short (minimum four-breath) meditation each day, and commit to using them. This might involve a single type of opportunity, such as, "Every time I walk to and from the bathroom, I will do at least four breaths' worth of walking meditation with breath-labeling and counting" (exercise 7). Or you could identify more than one type of opportunity, for a total of six: "Twice a day, as I walk from the front door to the garage or vice versa, and twice a day as I walk between the parking lot to the office entrance, and twice a day as I walk to and from the lunchroom to my cubicle, I will do at least four breaths' worth of walking meditation with breath-labeling and step-counting" (exercise 11).

The more you can make a habit out of doing a meditation exercise every time you are in a particular situation, the easier it gets both to remember and to do. You may even find, as I have, that what was once a mindless task becomes a tiny mental vacation. Most importantly, each time you do any of these exercises, you are building the mental muscle that will allow you to gain control over your thoughts and emotions.

A Few Variations on the Exercises

Just because these new variations and exercises come after the ones you've already learned does not mean they are necessarily more difficult to stay fully focused on. You may actually find some of them to be easier, but you won't know until you try them.

The seated variations will give you additional opportunities for meditation. Just look for those moments when you're sitting, and then instead of reading the newspaper, or indulging in negative self-talk about waiting for that slow bus or waiter—you'll have something useful and important to do!

Exercise 12: Variable Walking Meditation with Breath-Labeling and Step-Counting

What makes this one variable? Well, in exercise 10, you determined the average number of steps that you took during each exhale. Then, in exercise 11, you took that number of steps during each inhale and each exhale, labeling each breath's worth of steps like this: "in…two…three, out…two…three…," carefully matching your stepping and your breathing. In this version of the exercise, you will allow the length of each inhale and each exhale to be whatever is comfortable, and just count however many steps that takes, with no attempt to regularize either your breathing or your walking.

1. Stand up and exhale comfortably and completely.

2. Begin walking at a steady, medium-slow pace. Timing your foot to hit the floor just as you start your inhale, mentally label the first step with the word "in" exactly as that foot touches down. Label the rest of the steps during your inhale as "two" and "three" and so on—"in…two…three…four…" and so on until you are comfortably full of air.

3. As you start to exhale, label the out breath with each label word coming exactly as each foot hits the floor—"out…two…three…" and so on.

4. Continue to walk, breathe, and label. Don't worry if you have more steps during the inhale than the exhale, or vice versa. Just notice and label, don't control.

5. Experiment by walking faster or slower. Continue to observe two things: the direction of your breath, and the number of steps you take during each inhale and each exhale.

Important Instructions for When You Lose It

Now here's the critical part. When you lose your count, or forget to label a breath direction change—and I say "when" rather than "if," since we all lose it sometimes—do this: notice any negative thoughts that may arise ("I'm lousy at this"; "I can't do anything right"; "this is dumb") and *immediately* restart the exercise at the beginning of your next inhale: "in...two...three...four..." and so on.

In the long run, being able to notice that you've lost it, to leave the negative thought behind, and to return immediately to the exercise with full concentration will bring you to a deeper state of mindfulness than you'd be able to attain if you did the exercise perfectly from the beginning. Even if you can stay focused only for a single breath, if you can return to the next single breath's worth of meditation without negative thoughts wasting your valuable time, you are meditating, and building mental muscle.

Exercise 13: Seated "Walking" Meditation with Breath-Labeling and Step-Counting

Even the busiest of bees has to sit down sometimes, and this can provide a good opportunity to do a few minutes of meditation exercise. So I've created an exercise with enough kinetic action to keep your attention, even though it looks static and passive.

1. Sit up, with your back straight and both feet flat on the floor.

2. Simulate the act of walking in one of three ways. You can alternately press each foot flat against the floor in the same rhythm and speed that you'd use when walking at a steady, medium-slow pace. Your thigh muscles will move as you do this, so if you prefer to be more discreet, you can just bend the ends of the

toes of each foot down into the floor, alternating feet, to simulate a walk. Or you can tap each foot.

3. Then label and count as in exercise 12, as though you were actually walking: "in...two...three...four...five, out...two...three..." and so on.

If you'd prefer, you can use exercise 6, the seated meditation with breath-labeling and counting, when you happen to be seated for a few moments. Seize the moment—and meditate!

Exercise 14: Task-Based Walking Meditation with Breath-Labeling and Step-Counting

If you have not found the previous exercises to be too difficult, here's a new wrinkle that most meditators—even relatively experienced ones—often find challenging.

1. Choose a task of relatively short duration. It could be a made-up task, such as, "I am going to walk to the light switch, turn it off and then back on, and walk back to where I started."

2. As you do the task, perform a standard walk/breath/step count meditation: "in...two...three...four...five, out...two...three..." and so on, until your task is completed and you've returned to your starting point without losing track of breath-labeling or step-counting.

This exercise may prove harder than you thought it would be. Or, if it seemed easy, try experimenting with progressively longer and more complicated tasks.

Exercise 15: Task-Based Meditation with Breath-Labeling and Counting

A similar meditation can be performed while you do almost any task (though for most of us it gets much harder if there is any interpersonal contact during the exercise; we'll confront that issue later).

1. Choose a task that you do repeatedly, so that it takes little mental attention. I like to do this one when brushing my teeth or shaving.

2. Simply label and count each breath as "iiiinnn...one, ouuuttt one, iiinnn...two, ouuttt...two" until you get to four breaths. Then start again at "iiiinnn...one." Do as many sets of four breaths as it takes to complete the task.

Again, it's important that when you lose count or forget to label, you instantly return to "iiiinnn...one" without any self-criticism or other thoughts that are clearly not useful to this exercise. If a thought doesn't help you to stay focused on labeling and counting during the task, it is a "dead-end" thought; I'll tell you more about these in the next chapter.

Exercise 16: Harder Task-Based Meditation with Breath-Labeling and Counting

This exercise is the same as the last one, with one exception. Instead of labeling and counting your breaths up to four, then starting again, see how many breaths it takes you to complete the entire task.

1. Choose a really simple made-up task, as described in exercise 14.

2. Label and count your breaths until the task is done. How many breaths does it take you to complete the task?

Once you have successfully counted breaths during your made-up task, try it with a real task, like washing your hands.

As you become more able to stay focused on your meditation while conducting a simple task, do something that's a bit harder or that takes a little longer. Brushing teeth, washing a few dishes, shaving, showering, feeding the cat—these are all good tasks during which to meditate.

If this seems difficult, do it with shorter and easier tasks while you continue to work on exercise 15 (counting breaths to four only) with the harder tasks. And remember, when you mess up: no thoughts other than back to "iiiinnn...one..." and so forth. Okay?

Summing Up

- This may be a good time to take a break from reading and just work on integrating one or more of the exercises from this chapter into your daily life.

- Please think about what's easier for you to stay focused on, and what's harder. But don't worry about doing what's hard—if you need to, just stick with exercise 7 or exercise 11 until you can stay focused for four breaths' worth of time.

- If you can't yet stay focused for four breaths' worth of time, and you feel frustrated, please reread "Important Instructions for When You Lose It," above.

- You don't need to do all of the exercises, though you may want to try them all at least once. Remember those islanders from the beginning of this chapter: one good meditation was all they needed.

- Begin thinking about times, places, and situations that will give you opportunities to practice the exercises while you are going about your daily life. Please identify at least six such opportunities, and do at least one "four-breath" exercise during each of them every day, starting today.

- Experiment with the task-based meditations at the end of the chapter, but be aware that some tasks may be very difficult to meditate during. If you lose your focus, just start labeling and counting (from "innnn...one") again on your next inhale, leaving negative thoughts behind.

6

types of thoughts:
real-life, self-talk,
and dead-end

In chapter 5 you began to develop a customized mindfulness program, using the exercises that you've already learned. Now it's time to start thinking about three different kinds of thoughts that you'll need to learn to contend with as you build your meditation practice:

- "Real-life" thoughts are thoughts that arise in reaction to actual events: "There's a parking space."

- "Self-talk" thoughts are those that arise (as you can guess) when you're talking to yourself, whether consciously or subconsciously. Self-talk often occurs in response to either an actual event or a trigger thought.

- "Dead-end" thoughts are thoughts of any kind that occur repeatedly and serve no useful function.

Although there is quite a bit of overlap amongst these types of thoughts, having labels to go with them will help you identify them as they enter your mind—a very useful skill to develop, as it happens.

Real-Life Thoughts

Real-life thoughts arise in direct response to actual events; their purpose is to use the highly developed human brain to come up with skillful reactions to any situation. It can be a long-lasting, important event or a short-term, trivial one that we are reacting to. Perhaps the budget for your department is going to be cut by 30 percent this year. You'll need to do some planning and perhaps even grieving as you decide how to deal with the situation. Or, near the end of your lunch hour, you're at the end of a long checkout line, and the clerk is annoyingly slow. You'll need to do a quick analysis of the situation ("If I don't get beer for the party tonight, I'll have to stop at the liquor store on my way home, where it will be more expensive. But if I stay, I may be late getting back to work.").

Part of what defines a real-life thought (and makes it useful) is that once you've done all useful thinking on the real life event or issue, you then turn your attention to different things until either the situation changes (and thus must be reconsidered) or new information arises. This process is rather like a "proper" use of the fight-or-flight response. When the saber-toothed tiger leaps or a taxi heads at you, it is wonderful to have your fight-or-flight response there to help you defend yourself.

But if you spend every subsequent moment worrying about the return of the taxi or tiger, keeping yourself in a constant state of stress response, your life becomes a painful mess. Similarly, if you keep returning obsessively to a real-life thought ("How can they cut our budget like that?") or ("They should fire that clerk!") after you've completed all useful consideration of the situation, the once-useful real-life thought becomes a dead-end thought, a category of thought I'll discuss in a moment.

Self-Talk Thoughts

Self-talk is just what it sounds like: a monologue taking place inside your head. Try it right now. Tell yourself, without speaking, "I'm reading about self-talk thoughts right now." That's what I'd call a "neutral" self-talk thought: it's neither positive nor negative, just descriptive of what's happening. Self-talk can be neutral, positive, or negative.

Although talking to oneself can have negative social connotations, many of us use self-talk in a constructive way. For example, some people find that talking their way through an oft-repeated complex set of actions—like piloting a plane—helps them to remember the steps that are needed. Athletes and musicians often engage in positive self-talk before a game or concert.

Sadly, for many of us, self-talk tends to be both negative in tone and unintentional—even subconscious. We stumble walking into a room; the physical event triggers a self-talk thought: "I'm so clumsy." If self-talk has become a habit for us, we may combine self-talk thoughts, each more painful than the last, like links in a chain: "I'm so clumsy...everybody's looking at me...they think I'm stupid...I AM stupid...I hate myself."

The stumble itself did us no real damage, but the self-talk it triggered did. If it were a single occurrence, calling yourself clumsy or stupid would not matter so much. But if you are prone to negative self-talk, it's probably occurring on an ongoing basis, and increasing your levels of self-judgment, doubt, self-hatred, and possibly fear.

When we fail to complete a meditation exercise or to stay as focused as we'd like, negative self-talk often arises. This is a wonderful opportunity to notice the negative, counterproductive self-talk and immediately return our attention to performing the exercise. And in a very real way, many of the meditation exercises in this book could be described as a form of positive and productive self-talk—even if all you are saying to yourself involves counting or labeling steps or breaths. As you continue to build mental muscle (using "good" self-talk), you'll find it easier to notice all self-talk, evaluate it for positive or negative tone, and make it work for you rather than against you.

Dead-End Thoughts

Imagine that you're driving to a party on the other side of town. You've left just enough time to get there, but not much extra. You know that your destination is on a street parallel to the street you're on, and you're planning to turn right at the next large intersection. If you see a right-hand turn coming up with a large yellow and black "dead-end" sign at its entrance, are you likely to turn there? Of course not! And yet we often let dead-end thoughts beguile or grab or engross us.

A dead-end thought is a thought that you have explored as carefully as you need to in order to determine its complete lack of usefulness. If your ears are too large, but you don't plan to get an ear-cut, well…any further thoughts about your ears being too large are dead-end thoughts. If you can't stand a co-worker, but she's the boss's daughter, and you are unwilling to quit, dwelling on your dislike for her is likely to be a dead-end thought. Always be careful, though, that you don't label a thought a dead end just because it is unpleasant—that's denial, not a dead end.

Situational Dead Ends

Some dead-end thoughts are always un-useful. Others can be situational: a thought that is a dead end in one context may not be in another. Thinking about lunch during work is a dead-end thought. No value to it at all. And thinking about work during lunch (unless you absolutely have to) is only apt to reduce your enjoyment of what you're eating.

In addition—and this is important—any thought that enters your mind while you are doing a meditation exercise is a situational dead-end thought, unless it is directly related to the meditation (labeling breath, counting steps, and so on). No exceptions!

When Real-Life Thoughts Become Dead Ends

Some thoughts veer into dead-end territory when you can't seem to control their frequency. If you have an aging parent with health needs, or a child with problems, of course you need to do a certain amount of planning and researching and, perhaps, grieving about the issue (more on grief later). These are real-life thoughts. But if they arise so repetitively that they affect your mood or your ability to function (including your ability to deal with the situation), they become obsessive thoughts—and dead ends, for sure.

Self-Talk Dead Ends

Most negative self-talk thoughts are dead-end thoughts, too—or even chains of dead-end thoughts, with one leading to others that are even worse. Once we learn to understand and evaluate the self-talk process, we can learn to short-circuit or otherwise diminish its hold on us.

My Dead-End Thoughts

Perhaps hearing about a few of my own dead-end thoughts will help you to recognize some of your own. The following are what I call "chronic" dead-end thoughts—they've been around for a while, and are likely to remain in my head for a while (although I can choose not to pay attention to them).

- I'm a good fifteen pounds overweight, but not planning to diet anytime soon. (And the moment I do decide to diet, this will no longer be a dead-end thought for me.)

- My office is a mess. (But I can mostly find what I need to find in it, and neatness for its own sake is not a strong value of mine.)

- I have an ongoing dispute with someone; I can get very annoyed when I think about it. (But there is nothing practical that I can do to make things better between us, nor can I remove myself from the situation.)

What I call dead-end thoughts "du jour" involve situations that are annoying but of short duration—a bad hair day, an overtired child, mildly disappointing business news, and so on. In most of these situations, it doesn't take much deliberation to decide that allowing such a thought to linger in the mind can't provide any possible benefit.

Choosing a Dead-End Thought to Work With

Later in this chapter, I'll ask you to apply a meditation exercise to one of your dead-end thoughts; you may want to pick one now. Choose something that is clearly a dead end for you, using these criteria:

- It should be something that is slightly irritating *whenever* you think about it, not a situational dead end, like having lunch thoughts during work time. If you need to think very much about whether this thought has any positive use for you at all, choose another one.

- It shouldn't be your worst, super-stressor dead-end thought—that is, it should not produce significant or noticeable fight-or-flight symptoms.

- Just pick a mildly annoying, persistent dead end—something that you'd prefer were different, but that you can't or won't change, at least for the foreseeable future.

- You can use a self-talk chain as your dead-end thought. For example, if thinking of colleague X triggers a chain like "She's always late...she doesn't value my time...she shouldn't treat me like that...," go ahead and use it (if it's not too much of a stressor).

Got a dead-end thought? Good. You'll use it in chapter 7.

Labeling Types of Thoughts

Review the types of thoughts—real-life, self-talk, and dead-end—in the Summing Up section, below, and take a moment to list one or more of each type that inhabit your own mind. You'll use this list later on. If it seems difficult to come up with items for the list, look at my own list of dead-end thoughts, above. The first (overweight) and the second (office mess) are pretty standard-issue dead-end thoughts. The third is a self-talk dead-end thought.

Summing Up

- Being able to think is one of humankind's greatest assets, and also the source of some of our greatest pains.

- Understanding three common categories of thoughts—real-life, self-talk, and dead-end thoughts—will help you use mindfulness to deal more skillfully with the latter two types, which often produce stress responses.

- Real-life thoughts are useful, action-oriented observations and reactions to actual events.

- Self-talk thoughts are just what they sound like: talking to yourself. The content of your self-talk can be neutral, positive, or negative. Mindfulness helps us minimize negative self-talk while increasing positive self-talk. In fact, it's possible to argue that many meditation exercises are forms of beneficial self-talk.

- Dead-end thoughts are also just what they sound like. They take you nowhere useful. It can take some analysis to determine what is and what is not a true dead-end thought.

- Whenever you are doing a meditation exercise, *any* thought—pleasant or unpleasant—that is not part of that exercise is by definition a situational dead-end thought. As soon as you notice it, return your attention to the breath labeling, or the step counting, or whatever tasks that meditation exercise is composed of.

- Real-life thoughts, if they recur at inappropriate times, and self-talk thoughts, if they are negative, can become dead-end thoughts. Dead-end thoughts can be either chronic (you return to them repeatedly) or du jour (passing, one-time thoughts).

- Use the instructions in this chapter to choose a mild dead-end thought that you'd like to work with in the next chapter. You'll discover in upcoming chapters that removing just a few of your most common dead-end thoughts can go a long way toward reducing stress and improving your mental outlook.

7

four ways to use the meditation exercises

In the early stages of building a mindfulness practice, we put most of our time and energy into getting used to the meditation exercises and beginning to use them to help us deal more skill-fully with events in our lives and thoughts in our minds—includ-ing real-life thoughts, self-talk thoughts, and dead-end thoughts. We can do this in four ways. Later on, we may choose to look at more abstract mindfulness elements such as compassion, being present, and "nonduality" (the lack of a sense of division between one's individual "self" and the rest of the universe).

Way Number One: Building Mental Muscle

Building mental muscle is the first priority for the beginning student of mindfulness. Each time you do any of the exercises, for however long you do it, you build at least a bit of mental muscle. So in chapter 5 you began to identify convenient opportunities to do the exercises during the course of your daily life, and to use them to build mental muscle. But there are three additional ways these exercises can be used.

Way Number Two: Diverting Attention from Thoughts

As you learned from the walking and counting meditation with negative thought (exercise 2), turning your attention with strong focus onto a new object (in that case, counting the number of steps it takes to walk around a room) completely diverts your attention from a mildly negative thought. This technique can be a skillful, mindful way to deal with certain categories of un-useful thoughts. It should not be used to deny or avoid dealing with negative thoughts about situations that must be dealt with—that is, useful real-life thoughts. But dead-end thoughts—which have no redeeming social or psychological value for you—are great targets for this diversion strategy. Try the following exercise to see how.

Exercise 17: Dead-End Thought-Diversion Meditation

1. Begin walking at a medium-slow pace.

2. Bring to mind your chosen dead-end thought from chapter 6.

3. Count your steps until you reach the number twenty. Do this with great accuracy, making sure you don't lose your count.

What happened to the dead-end thought as you were counting steps?

If it mostly evaporated when you started counting your steps, it was a good choice (mild enough) for this exercise. If you like, practice this exercise with this particular dead-end thought a few times a day; you'll find it will begin to lose the ability to annoy you as much.

If the dead-end thought did not disappear or at least recede into the back of your mind, you may have chosen too strong a dead-end thought to use—for now at least. You have two options. You can return to this exercise with an even milder dead-end thought—one that bothers you only slightly. Or you can continue on with the thought you've chosen, using Way Number Three, turning attention toward the breath.

Way Number Three: Turning Attention Toward the Breath

When working with low-annoyance-level dead-end thoughts, it is often enough just to divert our attention from them using any kind of meditation, breath-based or not. Although annoying, they don't really produce full-fledged fight-or-flight reactions. When working with either a difficult real-life event or a thought (dead-end or not) that is capable of producing serious anger or fear, it's necessary to use the breath as a meditational focus, since that's what short-circuits the stress response. If the dead-end thought you worked with in exercise 17 did not diminish after you did that exercise—or if it was strong enough to actually trigger a stress response—you'll need to breathe your way through it.

Before you begin the following exercise, choose a thought that produces moderate fight-or-flight symptoms. This could be any type of thought—real-life, self-talk, or dead-end. As you recall, fight-response symptoms include tightening of fists and clenching of teeth, and flight-response symptoms include butterflies in the stomach, flinching or hunching of shoulders, and tingling in the scalp. Since you're using only a moderately stressful thought, these symptoms may be brief in duration and hardly noticeable. But they are there, if you look within for them.

77

It may also be helpful to spend a few moments reviewing and practicing exercise 7 or exercise 11 in chapter 4. If you like, you may also review exercise 12 (in chapter 5), which is another variation on a walking meditation with breath-labeling and step-counting.

Exercise 18: Breath Focus Meditation with Negative Thought

1. Begin walking at a medium-slow pace.

2. Bring your chosen stressful thought into your mind as you continue to walk for a minimum of 30 seconds. Allow enough time so you feel the thought's physical, fight-or-flight-response effects.

3. Once you've begun to experience the physical effects of the thought, however mildly, turn your attention to your breathing, noticing whether you are inhaling or exhaling.

4. As you finish your next exhale, and with the first footfall of your subsequent inhale, begin labeling and counting, using the techniques in one of the exercises you've just reviewed.

5. Continue staying as closely focused on the meditation exercise as you can for at least one minute.

How did changing your mental focus from the stressful thought to the meditation exercise change the way that thought affected you? Did the thought seem to disappear entirely? Did it seem to fade out as you began the meditation? Did it keep recurring, making it hard to stay focused? If this last was the case, it may be useful to choose a less stressful thought to work with, for now.

Way Number Four: Split Attention, and Desensitizing Ourselves to Thoughts

In addition to diverting our attention entirely from a thought, or turning our attention to the breath, we can also learn to split our attention between a real-life situation (or thought) and a meditation exercise. Doing this has two main benefits.

One benefit is that split attention can be used to desensitize ourselves to the effect that a dead-end thought has on us. The exercise below will demonstrate how to do that. It will also be good practice for the more difficult-to-attain benefit of split attention: during a difficult real-life situation (but one that will not be helped by either fighting or fleeing), splitting your attention in this way can prevent self-talk or other un-useful thoughts from causing a stress response.

Got an angry customer calling? Getting angry yourself probably won't help much—having a stress response in an already difficult situation is unlikely to be skillful!

Lots of diligent practice can even help you short-circuit stress responses in situations when a fight-or-flight response occurs instantaneously—but that's advanced-practice work, and will be discussed later in this book.

It's good to know about split attention and to start working on it, but it may be a while before you can do it successfully during a real-life event. That's why we'll begin our practice with your chosen dead-end thought.

Exercise 19: Dead-End-Thought Split Attention and Desensitization Meditation

In this exercise, you'll again combine your chosen dead-end thought with your favorite walking, counting, and breath-labeling exercise (choosing among exercises 7, 11, and 12). But this time, instead of attempting to keep all of your mental focus on your meditation—on your steps, or your breath labeling—you'll attempt to *alternate* between the dead-end thought and the meditation.

1. Begin walking at a medium-slow pace.

2. As you continue to walk, bring your chosen stress-ful thought into your mind. Allow just enough time so you begin to feel the thought's physical, fight-or-flight-response effects.

3. As soon as you've begun experiencing the physi-cal effects of the thought, turn your attention to your breathing, and notice whether you are inhaling or exhaling.

4. With the first footfall of your subsequent inhale or exhale (in other words, the very next time you change the direction of your breath), begin labeling and counting, using whichever meditation pattern is easiest for you to focus on.

5. Try to stay focused on that meditation pattern for about four breaths' worth of time.

6. Now return to step 2, bringing the dead-end thought back into your mind until you can feel it beginning to physically affect you.

7. Repeat the entire process from step 2 through step 6 a few times.

Ask yourself these questions: Did your dead-end thought involve self-talk? Or was it a single mental image or feeling? Was it difficult to shift gears from the dead-end thought to the meditation? Did you find yourself wanting to keep thinking or self-talking about the dead-end thought? Was it harder to make yourself leave the meditation and go back to the dead end?

This exercise—like so many others—gets easier with practice. If you continue to practice regularly and often, you'll find that when your dead-end thought arises spontaneously, it becomes easier and easier to banish it from your mind. And doing this exercise will help you build the mental muscle that will eventually allow you to short-circuit the negative effects of *any* thought.

Summing Up

- At this stage of building a mindfulness practice, there are four main ways to use the meditation exercises.

- Way Number One is to use the exercises to build mental muscle. That's a worthy goal all by itself.

- Way Number Two is to divert your attention from a mildly un-useful thought. This way works well with mildly annoying thoughts that don't trigger full-blown stress responses.

- Way Number Three uses a breath-focused exercise to practice short-circuiting the stress response. This way works for stronger un-useful thoughts that trigger fight-or-flight responses.

- Way Number Four involves splitting attention between a negative thought or event and a breathing exercise. You'll start by learning to alternate your focus between a chosen dead-end thought and your favorite breathing exercise. Over time and with practice, you will desensitize yourself to the dead-end thought. Eventually, you'll be able to short-circuit many or even most of your stress responses as they begin to occur.

8

nose, eyes, ears, hands...and other people

You've now learned a number of simple meditation exercises, and are, I hope, beginning to insert them into the fabric of your daily life during all convenient opportunities. And since most or all of the exercises can be done anywhere—sometimes even while you're doing something else—there should be many such opportunities. In this chapter I'll provide you with some additional exercises that will help you build mindfulness by training you to focus, at will, on different types of awareness. However, I'd be remiss if I did not issue, right here, a warning: If you are not making use of *at least* six opportunities a day to do one of the walking and breathing exercises, this method won't work for you. Sadly, no fitness method will provide even marginal benefits if you just read about it and don't actually do the walking, the weight lifting, or the Russian bell swinging. Neither will a mindfulness method, if you don't exercise enough to build mental muscle. If this admonition applies to you, please redouble your efforts. (And if you *are* doing your six a day—you can double your efforts as well, and go for twelve!)

A Bit More on Mindfulness

Back in chapter 1, I defined mindfulness as the state of mind in which we can choose to be fully aware on many different levels—physical, mental, philosophical—at once, or to alternately focus our awareness tightly on any of these various levels at will. So far, you've been spending most of your time focusing your awareness—your mental attention—on just a few physical things (like your breathing, or your steps). You've probably noticed that I've also been quite concerned about what you are *not* focusing on, like dead-end thoughts.

As you continue to build mental muscle through the meditation exercises, it becomes easier to stay focused on whatever you choose to stay focused on—that's pretty much the definition of mental muscle. Now I'll give you a few more things to focus on, some of which may be a bit more abstract than the ins and outs of breathing or the counting of steps. This may make them harder to focus on, but that's okay. You'll just get practice returning your attention to the meditation as soon as you've noticed thoughts drifting in—that's what builds the mental muscle.

How Well Do You Know Your Nose?

Unless you suffer from allergies or play a wind instrument, you may not pay too much attention to the difference between nose breathing and mouth breathing. This may seem like a strange or whimsical aside, but bear with me. Mindfulness is about the ability to control mental awareness—this often involves bringing awareness to areas that we don't usually focus on. Like the nose.

Imagine the doctor placing the cold end of her stethoscope on your back and saying, "Breathe through your mouth only, please." To do so you'd tighten muscles in the back of your throat that close the passage between nose and mouth. Should she (for some reason) ask you to breathe through your nose only without shutting your mouth, you'd raise the back of your tongue to close the passage between mouth and lungs, and all air would be directed through your nose. In the following exercise, you'll consciously focus your attention on this mouth/nose connection. (If you have a cold, or it's allergy season, you'll have to skip this one for now—sorry!)

Exercise 20: Mouth and Nose Breathing Meditation Variations

1. Sit comfortably and focus your attention on the connection between your nose and your mouth.

2. Take a breath through your nose. Try doing this in two ways: with your mouth staying open, and with your mouth staying shut. You'll notice that if your mouth is shut, you can nose-breathe without raising the back of your tongue. Now breathe through your mouth.

3. Inhale through your nose and exhale through your mouth. When inhaling, you can either keep your mouth closed, or keep it open and use the back of your tongue to keep air from escaping—try it both ways.

4. Continue until you've done half a dozen breaths.

5. Now reverse the exercise—inhale through your mouth and exhale through your nose.

Some people find that consciously changing the breath between nose and mouth for the inhale and exhale of a single breath requires sufficient mental concentration that few thoughts are able to intrude. If you find this to be the case, start looking for opportunities to do this exercise. With just a minute of practice, you can do it with your lips slightly parted, and it will be invisible to even the most careful observer.

If you find thoughts intruding more than when you are doing other meditation exercises, you may need to add another level of complexity to the process. Do this by counting and labeling your breaths as in exercise 6 (in chapter 4): "iiinnn [nose]...one, ouuuttt [mouth]...one, iiinnn [nose]...two, ouuuttt [mouth]... two," and so on. Go to four breaths and repeat, or ten—your choice. Still not a Bond flick, but pretty attention-grabbing for most people.

You can also do the nose/mouth breathing as part of a walking and breathing step-counting exercise. Most of us can move a lot more air per second through our mouth than our nose, so the variable walking meditation with breath-labeling and step-counting (exercise 12), in which we take however many steps we like during each part of the breath, will be easier to use for this. Just label your ins and outs, count your steps, and remember to alternate nose and mouth, and you can't go wrong: "in [mouth]...two...three, out [nose]...two...three, four... five...," and so on.

Are We Cheating Yet?

Some of you may be thinking that if I give you an exercise that involves walking, counting, labeling, and alternating nose and mouth breathing, how different is that, really, from the Bond movie? I've loaded you down with so many things to do that there's just no time to have any thoughts. Is it still meditation?

I would answer "yes." None of the tasks just mentioned are, in themselves, very compelling of attention. And my intent is to help you stay focused on them in such a way that thoughts unrelated to the meditation don't enter. Certainly, many meditation teachers are far stricter and more purist than I am. They might give you a single syllable, like "om," and tell you to sit and spend half an hour focusing on that alone. Or have you spend a few weeks concentrating on the philosophical sensation of "am-ness." Both of these wonderful meditation practices are not, in my experience, likely to work too well as beginning exercises for busy, kinetic, "bee" people like myself—or, perhaps, like you.

So this book starts with the simplest exercises possible, then presents progressively more subtle objects of meditation, in the form of exercises that we can do while we do other things (like walking from place to place, or sitting in front of a computer). We started out by counting steps, which any drunken pirate with a treasure map can do. We then moved on to labeling our inhales and exhales, and added other variations and refinements. Many of these exercises have involved, to paraphrase my definition of mindfulness, focusing on multiple objects of attention at one time: for example, breaths and steps, or counting and labeling. As you've got better and better at staying focused on more complex exercises, you've been building mental muscle.

The next exercise will require stronger focus skills still, since we are going to turn our attention to a process—the process of seeing—rather than the more concrete objects or single actions (breathing, stepping) that we've been using to focus on so far.

The Eyes Have It

Whether searching for game in the savannah in the remote past or crossing a busy street this morning, our species has always used its relatively acute vision and the fast processing power of its cerebral cortex to survive. In all of our previous meditation exercises, I've given you no explicit instruction as to what to look at, or for. I assume that when you're doing any of the walking exercises, you've been "watching where you're going." Now it's time to take a closer look at visual awareness.

Alertness versus Apprehension

The phrase I just used, "watching where you're going," is relatively neutral. It does not necessarily imply that the going is dangerous, but it does signal a need to be visually alert to some extent. The word "apprehension," however, implies some anticipation about dangerous or negative events that might occur. I'll use the term "watchfulness" to mean "very careful visual alertness without any apprehension." This is the kind of looking you'd use to navigate a busy but crossable street; the kind of looking with which a well-fed housecat watches a mouse hole. In the following exercise, you'll practice a form of split attention, staying focused both on your meditation and on the ongoing process of watchfulness.

Exercise 21: **Watchfulness Meditation**

1. Choose any one of the previous meditations that involve walking—I'd suggest exercise 7 or 11 from chapter 4.

2. As you walk and breathe, keep your eyes watchful: that is, maintain a sense of visual alertness.

3. Keep a wide and constantly moving focus. Don't allow your eyes to be caught by any particular thing at all, however interesting or attractive. Just notice whatever you see, then go on to look at whatever you see next.

4. Don't allow your mind to start telling you a story about anything you see, because any thoughts that may arise—such as liking ("oooh, that's pretty") or judging ("someone should clean out that gutter")—are likely to make you lose your focus, and your count.

   Fortunately, doing the walking meditation will help you avoid getting "caught up" in a distracting thought.

5. If any thoughts do arise as a result of your watchfulness (or for any other reason), you know what to do: after instantly returning your attention to your breathing, notice whether you're inhaling or exhaling and start labeling and counting—and watching—again.

Auditory Alertness

As with the eyes, it is possible to bring alertness without apprehension to the sense of hearing. When you're in a state of "auditory alertness," you are listening to whatever sounds are audible, without expecting any of them to be especially exciting or frightening. If this next exercise seems difficult, don't worry. It will get easier as you develop mental muscle—just like all the others.

Exercise 22: Auditory Alertness Meditation

1. Sit comfortably, and close your eyes, if you like.

2. Listen alertly. What's the loudest thing you can hear? What's the softest thing you can hear? Can you attach a name to each sound ("That's a car going by; that's a bird outside; that's the hum of the computer")?

3. Reread exercise 6 in chapter 3, the seated meditation in which you label and count your breaths in sets of four: "iiinnn...one, ouuuttt...one," and so on, to breath four.

4. Now actually *do* exercise 6 very briefly—just four or eight breaths' worth.

5. Now split your attention: while you are breath-labeling and counting, try to simultaneously maintain auditory alertness, but without naming the sounds or allowing

       any sound to trigger a thought that makes you lose your count.

6. If you find yourself paying too much attention to the sounds—and especially if you start mentally naming them ("Hey, there's that bird again"), refocus on the breath.

If you like, you can also do this exercise while doing one of the walking meditations, although many of my students find it easier to do while sitting.

Using Mudras

Although I am the creator of a specialized form of yoga called HarmonicaYoga™ (and that's not a joke, even if it sounds funny), and a regular if inflexible practitioner of hatha yoga, I know only a few of the yogic hand configurations known as "mudras." Each mudra is said to have certain qualities, and maintaining them while doing hatha yoga or meditating is believed to impart those qualities to the yogi or meditator. I don't use them too much in my own yoga practice, but I do find that using one or two common mudras during any kind of walking meditation helps me—and many of my students—stay focused.

To use my slightly simplified version of the "gyan" mudra (considered a mudra of peacefulness): while walking with your hands hanging loosely at your sides, gently touch the tip of each forefinger to the tip of each thumb, in whatever way is most comfortable for you. To use the "shuni" mudra (considered a mudra of patience), touch the tip of the middle finger to the thumb. Though it's not a conventional mudra, I like to walk with both the fore and middle fingertips of each hand touching my thumb tips. It's possible that this use of these mudras is simply a nonverbal or sign language form of positive self-talk. Using these mudras as I describe them also gives us another object to focus on as we meditate. Either way, it's worth trying any of your walking meditations with a mudra. If you find it helpful, keep doing it, and it will be one more inconspicuous way for you to maintain a sense of mindfulness.

Another Handy Tool for Meditators

I'd like to share with you another invention of mine that has been well received by my students.

As you may know, the brain is divided into two halves, or hemispheres. The right hemisphere generally controls the left side of the body, while the left hemisphere controls the right side of the body. Each hemisphere is also largely responsible for certain tasks and functions: *very* broadly, the left hemisphere is said to handle more analytically oriented tasks, while the right hemisphere controls more creatively oriented functions. The following exercise activates each side of the brain sequentially as you breathe; it can be done with any breathing meditation.

Exercise 23: **Right Hand, Left Hand Breathing Meditation**

1. Begin any of the walking or breathing meditations you have learned so far. As you inhale, clench one hand slightly, to a comfortable extent (not as though you were getting ready to throw a punch or clutch something). Or use the mudras I've described.

2. As you exhale, release the slightly clenched or mudra-ed hand, and clench or mudra the other hand. Repeat throughout the duration of your chosen meditation.

Experiment a little with this exercise, and ask yourself whether one hand "feels more appropriate" when clenched during the inhale (or during the exhale). If so, use that hand. If it doesn't matter, just choose one hand for inhaling and one for exhaling, and stick with that. Like the two-handed mudra, this is simply an extra technique that can help you maintain focus during a meditation exercise.

Mindfulness and Other People

Jean-Paul Sartre's best-known quotation is probably "Hell is other people." The truth of that statement depends to a large extent upon whom we spend our time with, but almost all of us have at least one relative, friend, or colleague who can be difficult to be with. A plethora of benefits results from using split attention exercises in which one object of your focus is a difficult person and the other your own breath. Instead of being forced to simply endure the person's company, you are building mental muscle. At the same time, you are desensitizing yourself to the person's negative effect on you, and what could be better? We'll cover this topic in more detail in later chapters; since dealing with negative folk can be quite stressful, we'll start here with an exercise that doesn't (quite) require a real, live antagonist.

Exercise 24: Annoying-Personality Split Attention Meditation

1. Turn on your radio, TV, or online computer radio or video.

2. Tune in to a show that you don't like, one you'd normally tune out as soon as you heard that particular annoying voice or saw that face.

3. Start doing any of your breathing meditations. You can be seated, or you can use a walking exercise, as long as you can still hear or see the show you've chosen.

4. Attempt to keep your attention split between the annoying stimulus on-air and your breath focus.

5. If you find yourself getting annoyed to the point of feeling fight symptoms (clenching fists, teeth, and so on), you need to pay more attention to your breathing meditation. If you find yourself losing track of the exasperating nonsense that the irritating person is

spouting, you need (ugh) to put a bit more of your focus on to the show.

6. Spend just one or two minutes doing this, three if you can stand it.

Many of us will find that the split focus will defuse what we might call the show's annoyance quotient, because the partial focus on the breath helps to prevent a full-fledged stress response from taking hold of us. Although this may not be your favorite exercise, it can be a very useful one, especially when applied to real-life situations rather than talk radio or TV.

Summing Up

*   Important: Make sure that you are identifying opportunities to do your chosen exercises, and that you're doing them at least six times a day. The more often you do them, the more mental muscle you will build, and the more useful your mindfulness practice will be to you.

*   Experiment with all of the new exercises in this chapter. Some may seem odd, but try them anyway. If you find them useful in helping you focus, keep doing them. If not, stick to your old favorites for now, and come back to these later.

- The watchfulness visual meditation and the auditory alertness meditation may seem difficult, since you are focusing on the slightly more abstract processes of seeing and hearing rather than on the walking, labeling, and counting that you've done before.

- When in doubt, don't quit—just return to the basics for a while, then try the more subtle exercises again later on.

- If you have any difficult people in your life, practicing the last exercise in this chapter is very likely to help you to deal with them more mindfully... eventually.

9

the bee's guide to
visualization

Many people are familiar with the term "the mind's eye"—a reference to our ability to produce mental images, or thoughts that take the form of pictures, at will. Consider your first car, your favorite bicycle, your best pair of shoes. An image springs into your mind, and you can observe it almost as though it were in front of you. This is a simple form of visualization.

Now think of a simple task that you perform every day: brushing your teeth, climbing onto the bus, feeding the dog. As you bring the task into the view of your mind's eye, observe the steps necessary to complete the task: reaching for the toothbrush, spreading the toothpaste on it, doing the molars, and so forth. This is visualization.

However, visualization doesn't have to be only of something we've already experienced. We can also visualize things that we'd like to happen—or that we fear will happen. Like self-talk, visualization can work to either help or harm us. The exercises in this chapter will do the former.

Thanks to the work of such writers as Mihaly Csikszentmihalyi and Charles Garfield (with whom I had the privilege of working on a project to bring volunteer counseling to dying and grieving clients), most serious athletes now understand that taking some time before a match or race to visualize oneself performing the athletic actions necessary to win appears to enhance performance in the actual event. This incredibly useful technique can also be a powerful tool in the pursuit of mindfulness. The exercise below will give you a taste.

Exercise 25: Meditation Visualization

In this exercise, we'll use visualization as a form of mental "rehearsal." In doing so, we are likely to find that it's easier to conduct, in real life, what we've rehearsed on the level of thought.

1. Think of a situation that provides an opportunity to do a walking or seated breathing exercise. Perhaps you

usually read the newspaper on the bus, or think about what you're going to order at the diner on your way there. (Choose a meditation opportunity you are not already using.)

2. Imagine yourself in that situation. Instead of picturing yourself reading the paper or thinking about lunch (as you'd likely be doing in real life), imagine yourself inserting a short walking or breathing meditation into that situation.

3. Try to make the visualization as real as possible, using as many of your senses as possible: feel yourself sitting on the bus seat; smell the exhaust; notice the coolness of the air conditioning; hear the sounds of the other passengers or the traffic. And make sure you clearly imagine yourself doing the exercise as you sit there: "iiinnn…one, ouuutttt…one, iiinnn…two, ouuuttt…two," and so on.

4. In fact, as you are imagining yourself doing the exercise, actually do the exercise: "iiinnn…one, ouuutttt… one, iiinnn…two, ouuuttt two…," so that the reality of the meditation and the rehearsal of the visualization are merged in your mind.

5. Make a mental commitment to bringing your visualized action into your real life.

6. When that opportunity arises—when you're sitting on the bus, or walking to the diner—use it as you've rehearsed doing.

The more often you practice the visualization, the more it will help you bring the act you have visualized into reality. Of course, your visualized act must be realistic. You can spend years visualizing yourself leaping over tall buildings in a single bound, but you still won't be able to do it. But if your goal—what you want to achieve—is realistic, the visualization will help you to achieve it. And that's the point of the next exercise.

Desensitizing Yourself to an Anticipated Event with Visualization

Near the end of chapter 7, you practiced using split attention to desensitize yourself to a chosen dead-end thought (exercise 19). In the next exercise you will visualize an event that has three qualities: a) it is likely to occur before too long; b) it is likely to be at least mildly unpleasant for you (that is, likely to produce some level of stress response, whether fight-based or flight-based); and c) it is an event that you think might be improved if you were able to apply a meditation exercise before, during, or after it occurs.

I find that the situation of having to wait annoys me, so I might choose "waiting for the bus" as my situation or event for this exercise. The bus *should* come every five minutes, but it doesn't, which bugs me. Impatient by nature, I often do this exercise when anticipating a phone call or a meeting with someone whom I find exasperating. I also use it in my hospice work, when I know that I'm going to encounter an interpersonal situation that is likely to make me frightened. If you are planning to use this exercise with a vexatious person as object of your mental focus, make sure you've already spent at least a few minutes with exercise 24.

Exercise 26: Anticipated Event Desensitization Meditation

1. Choose a mildly annoying, mildly frightening, or mildly upsetting event (for me, feeling "upset" usually combines elements of annoyance and fear). The event you choose should be one that is likely to occur.

2. Using the instructions from exercise 25, try to visualize the event as clearly as possible, so that you can mentally perceive the sounds, the sights, and the feel of the anticipated event.

3. Using the instructions from exercise 24, split your attention between your visualization (whether of the bus not coming on time, or the annoying person or phone call) and your focus on the breathing meditation of your choice.

4. As in exercise 24, if you find yourself getting annoyed to the point of feeling stress symptoms, pay more attention to your breathing meditation. If you find yourself losing focus on the visualization, you may need to repeat step 2 for a moment before returning to the split focus.

The more minutes you spend doing this (and they don't have to be done at the same time—three times for two minutes each will probably be more beneficial than doing it once for six minutes straight), the more likely you are to find two positive effects: First, due to the desensitization process, the actual event may be less stress-producing than it would have been otherwise. Second, you are more likely to find yourself able to do a split attention meditation during the actual event, since you have mentally rehearsed it in advance.

Summing Up

- Visualization is a powerful technique that is widely used in the fields of athletics and musical performance. It is an important tool in developing mindfulness.

- Like self-talk, visualization can be used for good (imagining good things happening), or for ill (imagining bad things happening). Your choice! (And by the way: imagining a bad thing happening that you handle well…is a good thing!)

- The more completely you can imagine a situation, involving as many physical senses as possible, the more effective your visualization will be.

- Use visualization to rehearse using mindfulness techniques in specific real-life situations. This rehearsal will help you to actually use them.

- Visualization can also be used to desensitize yourself to anticipated real-life situations. It can be especially useful when dealing with a difficult person—just rehearse in advance the act of splitting your attention between the person and your breathing exercise.

10

a few moments of mindfulness, then a choice

Now it's time to start putting a few more of the exercises together. This will help you get the feel of what slightly more subtle or higher levels of mindfulness feel like (while simultaneously building mental muscle, of course). You'll begin by using your mental muscle to switch the focus of your attention amongst different *objects* (walking and breathing). Then you'll experiment with switching the focus of your attention amongst different *processes* (although all of them will still be on the physical level: walking, breathing, counting, labeling, seeing, feeling, and hearing). Finally, you'll integrate *nonphysical processes* into your focus-switching meditations, including both thoughts (such as dead-end thoughts) and mental processes (such as "judging").

Review Some Newer Exercises That You're Going to Use

If you don't mostly remember how to do them, you might want to review the following meditations, since I'm going to ask you to do them in a moment:

- the breath focus meditation with negative thought (exercise 18), in which you switch focus, while walking, from your chosen dead-end thought to your favorite walking and breathing meditation

- the watchfulness meditation (exercise 21), in which you maintain a state of visual alertness while doing your favorite walking meditation

- the auditory alertness meditation (exercise 22), in which you focus on the sounds you can hear, while doing a breathing meditation; if you have not done this one while walking, try it now

- the right hand, left hand breathing meditation (exercise 23), in which you clench one hand as you inhale, then clench the other as you exhale

Review the Basics

I'm assuming (and hope I'm correct) that you've got the three basic walking and breathing meditations down pretty well by now. If that's not the case, please go back and spend some time with them—you will need to use them here. They are:

- the breathing meditation (exercise 5), in which you just label breath parts ("iiinnn" and "ooouuttt");

- the walking meditation with breath-labeling and counting (exercise 7), in which you label each inhale and exhale and count each breath: "in…one, out… one, in…two, out…two," up to four, then start over;

- the walking meditation with breathing and step-counting (exercise 11), in which you label each inhale and exhale and count each step but simply allow each breath to take as many steps as it does: "in…two…three…four, out…two…three," for example.

Here's a meditation that will help you to review these three basic, important exercises while building lots of mental muscle and practicing subtle shifts of attention.

Exercise 27: Triple Breathing Walking Meditation

1. Do a minute or two of exercise 5, just labeling "iiinnn" and "oouuttt" parts of the breath. Don't try to coordinate your breathing with your steps, but allow this to occur if it does so naturally.

2. Then switch, without changing your pace, to a few moments of exercise 7, labeling inhales and exhales while keeping count of your breaths up to four: "in… one, out…one, in…two…" Do at least two sets of four breaths.

3. Again switch, without changing pace, to exercise 11, still labeling breaths but this time counting steps rather than breaths: "in…two…three…four…five, out…two… three," and so on.

Think about this exercise. Did one type of meditation seem easier than the others? Was it harder to stay focused when you were switching from one to another than when you used only one at a time?

I've found that, for us bees, using a variety of exercises and changing rapidly between them often helps us to stay focused. The following exercises are based on that conclusion. I'll ask you to please try them all. But even if you did only exercise 27, finding numerous opportunities throughout the day to practice it while walking from place to place, the mental muscle it produced would make a tremendous difference in your ability to avoid dead-end thoughts and short-circuit stress responses at will.

Exercise 28: Combined Eyes, Ears, and Hand Meditation

In this exercise you'll combine a focus on three different types of physical awareness while doing the breathing meditation (Exercise 5). As you no coubt recall, in this one you simply label each inhale with the mental label "iiiinnn" for as long as that inhale lasts, and label each exhale with an "ooouuttt" for as long as the exhale lasts. Try to concentrate your attention primarily on your visual, auditory, and muscular (clenching or doing mundras) sensations, while maintaining just encugh attention on the breath to be able to keep on labeling those "iiinnns" and "oouuttts" as you inhale and exhale.

1. Begin walking at a moderate pace, then start labeling your in and out breaths as per exercise 5.

2. After half a minute or so, add perhaps another half a minute of watchfulness meditation (exercise 21), with most of your attention going out through your eyes. Do this while avoiding thoughts to the best of your ability.

3. Then switch most of your attention away from your visual sense to your auditory sense, and do a moment of auditory alertness meditation (exercise 22). As soon as that gets difficult to maintain (in other words, when thoughts start to enter your mind)...

4. Return your attention to labeling your breaths, this time with the right hand, left hand meditation (exercise 23).

5. Repeat steps 1 through 4 at least one more time, preferably more.

Exercise 29: Combined Mindfulness Meditation

In this exercise you'll combine three different levels of mindfulness meditation: a walking and breathing exercise, a watchfulness exercise, and a dead-end thought exercise. Just give it a try now, and I'll tell you why it's important afterwards.

1. While walking at a moderately slow pace, begin with about a minute of either a breathing meditation (exercise 7), labeling each inhale and exhale and keeping count of your breaths up to four, when you'll start over…

    …or a minute of a walking meditation with breath-labeling and step-counting (exercise 11): "in… two…three…four…five, out…two…three," or whatever count fits your breathing and walking speed.

    Your choice. Don't obsess about how long you do it for—it could be forty seconds, or ninety.

2. Without stopping your walking and breathing exercise, add a watchfulness meditation element. Keep your eyes alert and your focus wide and constantly moving, not allowing any one visual image to capture your attention. Do this for half a minute or so.

3. Now jump your attention away from your eyes, your breath, and your walking to focus on your chosen dead-end thought from exercise 18. Stay with it long enough to notice tightness in the jaw, clenching of fists, or any anxiety.

4. Use your mental muscle to return to step 1, the breathing or breathing and step-counting meditation. Repeat the entire exercise at least once, and preferably a few times.

This is a demonstration of mindfulness in motion. In this exercise, we control the focus of our mental attention and change it at will, from breath to visual watchfulness, from visual watchfulness to dead-end thought, then back to breath. We have consciously shifted our attention from the level of simple physical processes (breathing, walking) to a more complex physical process (watchfulness) to the level of thought (dead-end thought), then back to the level of the original physical exercise of walking and breathing.

Just Looking, Just Listening

Since the following are not new exercises, but rather new ways of thinking about previous exercises, I won't number them. But they are still important, since they demonstrate a slightly higher form of mindfulness, which we can now begin to work on.

Do a moment of walking meditation with watchfulness, right now. Your eyes are receiving physical inputs, then sending them along the optic nerve into your brain, which is interpreting them on the fly. Tree. Sidewalk. Trash can. Does your mind start telling you a story about any of the visual inputs it receives? "Hmm, that tree needs pruning. And the trash can is overflowing." Well, you know what to do. Just return your attention to the walking meditation exercise, since by definition any thought of any kind that arises during a walking meditation (other than labeling the breath and/or counting steps) is a dead-end thought.

Do the same thing with the auditory alertness meditation, combining it with a walking and breathing meditation. Do thoughts enter your mind? Stay focused on your breath, your steps, and any sounds you may hear, without naming them.

This state of sensory alertness (which I hope you achieved for at least a few seconds interspersed throughout the exercises) is called by some of my mindfulness teachers "just looking," or "just listening." In this state, your mind is quieted enough by the breath focus so that it doesn't rush to judgment or tell those endless stories: "I like this sight; I don't like that sound; Oh, that reminds me of the tree I hit with my car in 1998."

Now try the same watchfulness meditation, but with a simpler breathing meditation, exercise 5, just labeling each "iiinnn" and "oouuttt." This time, you don't need to think about counting your breaths or your steps. It may be slightly harder to avoid self-talk about what you see, since the breathing exercise is simpler. But as you work on it, you'll find it easier to be "just looking" or "just listening" as you walk and label your inhales and exhales.

After some practice with the previous exercise—perhaps in a day, or a week, or a month—try "just looking" for a moment *without* doing *any* breath labeling. It will be harder to avoid self-talk, since a higher level of mindfulness and more mental muscle are required to stay focused on "just looking" without the aid of breath labeling. It may help to first do a moment of "just looking" with breath focus before you let go of the breath focus. Just stop the breath labeling, without adding any self-talk. Simple, right? But perhaps not easy.

To the outside observer, it looks like you're merely another person out for a stroll. But as an intrepid explorer of mindful action, your internal state is quite different, and you will know and feel it.

Just Doing

If you spend some time practicing these exercises, you'll be able to apply a similar focus of attention to "just doing" anything. When you are "just doing," all of your attention is focused on the task at hand, whether it is a hobby, a piece of work, an athletic or musical pursuit, or an interaction with other people. Basically, you pay attention only to what you need to pay attention to. This may change from moment to moment—as you are building the model airplane, you may need to attend to the baby's needs, and your attention will shift completely to doing that, then come back to the model plane when you return to it. While conversing with a friend, with full attention, you may have to take a call from a child or parent—and you will give that your full attention, as well.

As you grow to trust yourself not to allow your mind to catch you up in habitual fears, grievances, angers, and other stresses, you will put your attention where it's needed, when it's needed. This is hard to do well. It's hard to do at all. Most people never think of trying. But when you know that it's possible, and have some of the mental muscle needed to separate the mental chaff from the wheat—the habitual useless thoughts from the useful attention—you can start working on it. You may as well start now: building a mindfulness practice is the work of a lifetime.

The Cool Tongue Breathing Technique

This isn't really an exercise, but something you can use to add an extra element of physical perception to any of the breathing meditations. It's similar to a technique used in Kriya yoga.

Touch the roof of your mouth with your tongue, perhaps a quarter or half an inch back from your upper front teeth. Keep your tongue muscles loose, and make sure plenty of air can pass around the sides of your tongue as you breathe through your mouth. Simply notice the sensation of coolness on the underside of your tongue as you inhale. Exhale through either nose or mouth, as you like, but always inhale through the mouth. For those of us who are sensitive to physical sensation, this simple technique may help us keep focused during any walking or seated breathing meditation.

Before going on to the next chapter and facing the issue of judging, I'd like to give you another breathing exercise—something to do while seated anywhere, whether in front of the computer or waiting for lunch. If done carefully, this exercise exemplifies a deeply mindful state.

In this exercise, we pay even closer attention to our breathing process, rather than just noticing when we change the direction of our breath. For example, when we are breathing slowly and easily (as when our bodies are at rest), there will often be a moment of equilibrium between the inhale and the exhale. For a fraction of a second, the diaphragm muscle that flexes to force air into and out of our lungs is in a resting position. Please try this exercise. It will bring you to a deeper focus on the breath.

Exercise 30: Deep, Mindful Breath Meditation

1. After sitting quietly for a moment so that your breathing is as regular and slow as it usually gets, take a moderate inhale. Before you get *too* full, stop inhaling.

2. Notice that there are three ways to do this:

    You can keep your mouth open, while using the muscles in the back of your throat to close off your nose (as you learned to do in exercise 20) and raising the back of your tongue to stop air from escaping through your mouth.

Or you can shut your mouth and use the nose-closing muscles at the back of the throat to close your nose. This is what you'd probably do if you were underwater and trying not to breathe water into your lungs.

Or—and this is what I'd really like you to practice—you could simply "stop breathing" for a second or two. Allow the diaphragm muscle to relax at the end of a partial inhale (so you have plenty of oxygen), keeping your mouth and nose still open. (Practice this for a moment, putting your hand over the center of your stomach; you should feel no movement of the diaphragm. It's a bit like a sigh: relatively full inhale, nothing happening for a moment, then deep, slow exhale.)

3. Now breathe for a minute or two, making sure each inhale doesn't fill you up too much.

    At the end of each inhale, stop all diaphragm motion for a second or two, then exhale moderately but not completely.

    At the end of the not-full-exhale, pause. There should be no diaphragm motion yet—no inhale. After a second or two, begin your inhale.

4. Continue to breathe like this for a while, now labeling each part of the breath: "iiiinnn…pause, oouuuttt… pause, iiiinnn…pause, oouuutt," and so on.

Begin also to notice and label any other aspects of your breathing: a hiccup, a sneeze. As always, if you lose your focus and find that you are no longer labeling, return without even a fraction of a second's pause for self-talk ("I blew it! I can't do this!"), notice where you are (inhale? pause? exhale?), give it the proper label, and keep going.

Exercise 31: Slow Breathing Meditation

I find this exercise to be very compelling of attention, and I practice it to a degree that some would consider a bit extreme. Using a wristwatch or digital clock, I slow my breathing to the lowest comfortable speed (measured in seconds per inhale and exhale) that I can easily maintain for three to ten minutes without feeling oxygen-deprived.

If you are under the care of a physician or suffer from any breathing issues or disabilities, you *must* describe this exercise to your doctor and ask permission before trying this. Also: don't push yourself. The goal is to slow your breathing down to your slowest *comfortable* level, not to starve yourself of oxygen!

1. Sit quietly for a moment, then turn your attention to your watch or clock. Notice the speed with which the seconds change (this is easier with a digital clock, but doable with a clock with hands). As you finish an exhale, begin to count seconds: three for each inhale, then three for each exhale.

2. Label as you would when doing the walking meditation with and breath-labeling and step-counting (exercise 11), except that instead of counting your steps, you are counting off the seconds as they pass on

117

your clock: "in…two…three, out…two…three." This will slow your breathing rate down to ten complete breaths per minute, a slow but not extreme rate.

3. Try to time the speed of your inhales and exhales so that your lungs are comfortably full when you reach the count of three on the inhale and comfortably empty when you reach the count of three on the exhale.

4. If it feels as though you are running out of air, try "in…two, out…two"—one complete breath every four seconds, or fifteen breaths per minute.

5. If the three-count seems easy, try four seconds per inhale and four seconds per exhale: "in…two…three… four, out…two…three…four."

After some practice and experimentation, your goal will be to find the number of seconds per inhale and per exhale that is comfortable for you but requires total concentration in order not to get too full or too empty before your desired number of seconds is reached. For me (a blowhard), fifteen seconds on the inhale and fifteen seconds on the exhale (two breaths per minute) forces me to stay very concentrated. If my mind wanders for even a second and I don't control my speed of inhale or of exhale during that time, I run out of air before the fifteen seconds are up.

You may find that you need more time on either the inhale or the exhale. I often do the exercise with a longer inhale (twenty seconds) than exhale (fifteen seconds). Why? Because it feels right. If I'm in good aerobic shape, I'll sometimes even slow down to twenty-five seconds in and twenty out. But don't be competitive about this. The idea is to eventually find *your* slowest breathing rate that requires total focus but is not uncomfortable to maintain for three to five minutes. Once you find it, taking even a single breath at that rate will both build mental muscle and short-circuit stress responses.

Summing Up

- Combining a variety of meditation exercises and doing them sequentially is a great way to get the feel of mindfulness. In fact, doing this *is* mindfulness.

- We bees often find that doing more than one type of meditation in a single session (even if it's only a few minutes long) can help us to stay focused.

- The triple breathing walking meditation (exercise 27) is a great example of this. If you did only this exercise every time you had the opportunity to walk from one place to another, it would soon transform the way you think and feel.

- Once you are able to combine meditations that work with simple physical events (such as counting or labeling breaths and steps), more complex physical processes (such as seeing and hearing), and mental events (such as bringing dead-end thoughts into the mind and dismissing them at will), you are practicing mindfulness.

- This does not mean you can quit doing the basic mental muscle exercises, though!

- The ability to look around you without allowing thoughts to arise or allowing your mind to tell you stories about what you are seeing (called "just looking") is an important part of being mindful. When you can achieve this kind of calm attention with any type of action or task, it's called "just doing." It is at the heart of a mindful life.

- The last exercise in this chapter (slow breathing) is great for focus, although you'll need to see a watch or clock to do it. Don't be competitive or self-punishing though, and read the instructions carefully before trying it.

judging

Judging is the act in which we perceive something, whether thought, process, or external object, and assess its value in the form of self-talk. Many of us are prone to doing this, so many that the popular Myers-Briggs personality assessment uses the tendency to judge as one of four main ways to categorize people. In this typology (in very simple terms), some people are "perceivers"—they tend to notice things or events without instantly feeling the need to evaluate or analyze them; others are "judgers," habitually forming an opinion about each item that appears in their mental purview.

The dichotomy between judging and perceiving is very real. Often, judging is such an integral part of our personality that we don't even notice we're doing it. So identifying judging and its self-talk brings it into the light of day. This process of discovering then investigating what has been hidden or subconscious is a crucial component of mindfulness.

Self-Talk on Purpose

And now for something completely different—an exercise in which I ask you to indulge in a mostly negative form of self-talk: judging. Most of us do it at least some of the time, saying to ourselves, "I like this, don't like that, those are okay." Although value judgments are useful in some situations—I wouldn't want to buy a computer without making some—the fact is that the more we judge other things, the more we tend to judge other people—and ourselves.

Exercise 32: Like, Dislike, Neutral: Judging Meditation

I'd like you to try something that probably won't seem like a meditation exercise to you—it's more like what most of us do most of the time without prompting.

1. While walking, let your eyes wander around your environment, focusing on each thing you see for just

long enough to make a quick judgment about it in the form of self-talk—positive, negative, or neutral—before going on to judge the next item. "I like that flower. That bush? Neutral. Don't like that garbage smell. Like the blue sky through the trees. Loud motorcycle, ugh. Nice Porsche."

2. Sometimes self-talk other than a quick like, dislike, or neutral judgment arises: "Oooh, a Porsche, it's a 912, I wish I had one, that rich guy I used to work for did…." That's your cue to return to the quick judgment mode. If it seems hard to let go of the lengthier self-talk, instantly use your mental muscle to do a few breaths of exercise 11: "in…two…three…four…five, out…two… three…four," then return to judging mode.

Doing this in a mindful way—that is, being fully aware of what we're doing while we're doing it, instead of doing it by habit and beneath the level of self-awareness, can be very enlightening— and often helps us notice when we're doing it unconsciously. Until I learned to do exercises of this type from my revered teachers Stephen Levine and Jack Kornfield, I just didn't notice how my mind was a constant flurry of judgments. And some of the worst ones were about…me (but more on that later).

Exercise 33: Visual Judging/Nonjudging Meditation

1. Spend a moment doing your watchful walking meditation (exercise 21). Focus on steps, breath-labeling,

and visual alertness as usual, with no mental stories about what you're seeing. Your eyes are comfortably wide open, your face relaxed as you…just look. Just walk. Just look and walk.

2. Now switch gears. Stop all breath focus. Use self-talk to make negative mental judgments about as many items as you can, as soon as you perceive them visually. Look for things you can judge, and try to be quick, if not always accurate: "What an ugly bush. The sky is too gray. That dog's a fleabag." Tense the muscles under your eyes as you make these judgments, as though you're narrowing your eyes and wrinkling your nose at all you see. I clench my teeth slightly when making negative judgments—it helps me to be snarkier.

3. Loosen the muscles of your face and jaw, and return to your watchful meditation for a minute.

4. Now try a moment of "just looking." If you need help keeping thoughts from your mind, do a simultaneous exercise 5, just labeling "iiinnnn…oouuttt" as you breathe.

What does it feel like to go from constant, critical judging to "just looking?" For most people who try this exercise, it reminds them of how unpleasant an ongoing focus on the negative can be. And how letting go of it for a moment is like putting down a heavy burden. Being aware of the cost of habitual negativity may help you modify it—and you know how: bring the focus to the breath to stop self-talk in its tracks.

Judging Versus Analysis

Sometimes it's necessary to make decisions between options. I prefer to call this kind of thought "analysis" or "decision-making," using "judging" as a more negative and critical or fault-finding term. In terms of the types of thoughts described in chapter 6, we may treat judging as dead-end thought, while accepting useful analysis or decision-making as real-life thought.

Judging can trigger additional self-talk which results in a stress reaction: when "I don't like that" leads to "That's a bad thing for me" and perhaps "They shouldn't have done that." In the next chapter, we'll look at the types of self-talk that trigger these responses. The practice we're doing here in switching our attention from a judging mode to an observing or perceiving mode (with the use of a breath focus if necessary) will prepare us to short-circuit them.

Self-Judging

If we tend toward judging, we're likely to judge ourselves. In these days of mass media, this can be painful, as we compare our looks to those of the people we see on TV, our wallets to those of the super-rich we read about, our physical abilities to those of professional athletes, and our wardrobes to those in the pages of fashion magazines. As a result, not surprisingly, we see ourselves as lacking.

If you are a victim of rampant self-judging, you might want to begin by choosing a single piece of self-judgment ("Just about everyone is better-looking than I am") and declaring it a dead-end thought. If you've used the meditation exercises in chapter 7 to build the mental muscle needed to deal with dead-end thoughts, eradicating that first self-judgment can lead to ridding yourself of another, and another.

Of course, if there is some truth in your self-judgment (if you say, "I'm lazy," and you are), then you should explore the thought and decide whether you need to make changes in your life based on it. It's then no longer a dead-end thought, but a decision-making thought that can provoke positive action rather than a stress response. (Note: I write this as though it is easy. It's not. That's why we build mental muscle: to help us accomplish the difficult things that need doing.)

The Worst Kind of Judging

Perhaps the least productive kind of judging occurs at the moment when we have hopelessly lost count of our breath, or find ourselves labeling an exhale with an "iiinnn." At that point, we may indulge in self-talk such as "I can't do this!" or "I have the mental muscle of a banana slug." These are indisputably dead-end thoughts. Yet if we can use this moment to notice what we're doing and return our attention to even the simplest of the exercises (such as exercise 1), we can turn what seems to be a defeat into a victory for mindfulness.

Summing Up

- "Judging" is one of the most common forms of self-talk. By experimenting with it mindfully in low-stakes situations (as in exercise 32), we can learn to identify it.

- Once we begin to notice judging tendencies—and especially self-judging tendencies—we can choose a particular example of judging and treat it as a dead-end thought, as in chapter 7.

- Judging is especially destructive when we apply it to our meditation and mindfulness practice. However, if you can completely blow a meditation exercise, smile at your failings, and instantly return to the count or label of the next breath or step, you are being eminently mindful!

12

how to see it coming
before it hits the fan

Let's face it: many things, from an infection to an insurrection to a tired child's meltdown, are easier to deal with the earlier we notice them. Stress responses, and the inappropriate behavior they often cause us to display, are no different. Since stress response symptoms are caused by an increased flow of stress hormones produced by the fight-or-flight response, the sooner we can turn off the faucet, the less intense the symptoms—including our experience of anger and fear.

Consider the metaphor of my chapter title, above. Some noxious object is heading toward the fan. If we can somehow block it and deflect it onto the floor or move the fan before it is splattered by the blades, it will be much easier to clean up. In the case of mindfulness practice, the noxious object is likely to be nothing more substantial than a thought.

Thoughts as "Objects" in the Mind

We're very used to manipulating objects in the physical world. You can pick up this book, open and close it, read the words, or place it on a shelf until you find you need it.

Back in chapter 6, you began to consider the concept of dead-end thoughts, and chose one to work with. In chapter 7, with exercises 17, 18, and 19, you used different strategies in working with that dead-end thought: diverting your attention from it with a step-counting exercise; turning your attention from it to your breath; and splitting your attention between breath and dead-end thought so as to begin to desensitize yourself to the thought's effects. The thought became, like this book, an object that you could view and manipulate in various ways—ways that would reduce its ability to influence your stress hormone levels, your emotions, your actions. Perhaps you've also started to consider some judging thoughts, identified as such in the previous chapter, that you'd like to give this treatment to.

You Are What You Think?

There is a saying: "You are what you eat." Are you also what you think? Perhaps, but only to the extent that you allow your thoughts to control you. And the sad fact is that many of us do allow it—myself all too often included. This is perhaps the central issue of mindfulness.

Before we begin to explore mindfulness, the thought of our least favorite person or situation can trigger an instantaneous reaction of anger or fear or both. Yet it's possible to have that thought arise, notice that it is beginning to cause stress symptoms, and turn our attention to our breath, short-circuiting the stress response. We've practiced that already, with our dead-end thought. And what made that possible? Identifying the problematic thought in advance. It is thus possible—and advisable—to begin to recognize types of thoughts or situations that are likely to produce a stress response, and to prepare for them in advance.

A Slightly Higher Level of Mindfulness

Focusing attention on thoughts and thought processes is a slightly more subtle level of meditation than focusing on breathing or walking. Instead of using simple and repetitive labels such as "in" and "out," or numbers to count steps or breaths, we begin to attach descriptive labels to the common types of thoughts that inhabit our heads.

By observing our inner landscape as clearly as we observe the external objects of our lives, we gain control over it. Gain control, that is, if we've been building sufficient mental muscle by using the simpler exercises diligently, and if we've identified thoughts or events that are relatively likely both to occur, and to cause stress responses.

We can choose to turn our attention onto a thought or away from it. An event occurs (the bus is late) that would in the past have caused a sequence of negative self-talk ("My friends will be annoyed. This is going to ruin our plans! That stupid bus! I was stupid not to leave earlier!"). Instead, we've already identified this type of event as a common stressor and practiced treating the self-talk that it generates as a dead-end thought—we've seen it coming and deflected it before it could hit the fan.

Making a List of Recurring Negative Thoughts and Events

It's useful to start creating a list of your own most frequently recurring negative thoughts and events, with the object of practicing, in advance, the act of short-circuiting the stress responses these thoughts (or events) predictably cause. Start with just one or two items of each type of thought/event described below;

think of the list as a work in progress. Here are general types of thoughts/events that are often troublesome to many of us; perhaps you can think of some categories of your own as well.

Common Types of Dead-End Thoughts

Dead-end thoughts, you'll recall, are thoughts that have no positive use to us. These may be chronic dead ends (thoughts about being overweight, or about the mess on our desk) or situational ones (lunch thoughts during work, or work thoughts during a family event).

Don't forget to look for thoughts involving unpleasant sensations such as anger, revenge desires, blaming, and feeling unappreciated. Remember also to carefully investigate each thought before you classify it as a dead end, asking yourself where it came from, when and why it arises, and what it means to you.

Pleasant Thoughts and Daydreams

Pleasant thoughts can also be dead ends. I used to waste significant amounts of time in fantasizing about unlikely events—from having glamorous movie stars fall in love with me to winning the Nobel Prize. Entertaining, but more useful was looking at why I needed such fantasies, then applying mental muscle and compassion to those needy places. Needing these thoughts less gives me more time to spend on more important mental exercises and explorations.

Planning Thoughts: Useful and Un-useful

Thoughts in which you plan for future action can be dead-end thoughts, as well. It's important to think about what wood you're going to use to build that table, but it's a dead-end thought to have while having breakfast with the kids. And you have to think about how much you're willing to pay for that used car you're going to see on Monday, but once you've decided upon the number, continuing to think about and hone your decision may be more an obsessive (dead-end) thought than a useful one.

Negative Thoughts That May Not Be Dead Ends

Some thoughts may be painful, but to dismiss them entirely would be denial. In this case it can be useful to have a single phrase or sentence of self-talk that you can use to deflect the thought without denying it. If you hate your job and are looking for a new one, but the "I hate my job" thought arises while you're at the beach making a sand castle with your children, you might use the prepared self-talk response, "Yes, my job is awful. I am looking for a new one, but it is not useful to think about this right now." Once you deliver the response, use mental muscle to turn your attention first to a short breathing meditation, then back to the beach and your children. This is not denial, because when you are in the appropriate time and place you will put mental and physical energy into your job search.

Making yourself aware of thoughts of this type and crafting self-talk responses for them will allow you to diffuse the stress of the thoughts when they arise in inappropriate situations.

Difficult Events and People

Making a short list of difficult events and people—a meeting with the accounting department, say, or a phone call with your mother—will allow you to use exercise 26 in chapter 9 to desensitize yourself to them. Simply begin doing the meditation of your choice, then bring a visualization of the anticipated event into your mind, splitting your attention between the two different objects of focus (the event and the meditation). You can also, if it is easier, alternate your focus of attention: think about the difficult event, then use mental muscle to refocus on your breathing, then change back to the difficult event, and so on. This will prepare you to make this same shift during the actual event.

Naming Your Thoughts

As you come up with your lists of thoughts, it may be useful to give some of the most recurrent ones names. If you often think of Mr. Dithers, your boss, name that type of thought a "Dithers Thought." If you have a tendency to obsessively think and rethink your upcoming travel plans (after they've been decided upon), name that type of thought an "Obsessive Travel Plan Thought."

Exercise 34: **Thought-Naming Meditation**

This exercise is not so much a meditation in itself as an element that can be added to any of your other meditation exercises. It will help you learn to treat thoughts as objects that can be manipulated just like any other objects.

1. As you do any of your favorite exercises, thoughts will sometimes arise and distract you.

2. Normally, my advice is to return to the meditation focus as soon as you notice that a thought has intruded upon it.

3. In this variation, try to give the thought a short descriptive name: "Need to Fix the Roof Thought;" "Annual Review Thought," "Not Enough Money Thought," and so on. Perhaps you've already named a particular type of thought as you made your list of thoughts. If not, create a new name on the spot, then return to your meditation.

It's Your Choice Now

In the next few chapters I'll discuss some of the more advanced levels of mindfulness: subjects such as compassion, being present, and nonduality. This is all material that you'll want to think about if you're at all serious about the study of mindfulness itself. It's now time for you to make a choice about how you want to continue using this book: "just" hone the tools you've developed and customize them for specific situations in your life; or hone the tools while investigating deeper levels of mindfulness as well.

You see, the simpler elements of mindfulness—building mental muscle, avoiding dead-end thoughts, alleviating the stress response, desensitizing yourself to difficult people and situations—are excellent tools and techniques that will improve your daily life if practiced conscientiously. Yet they are principally the *means* to a mindful life, not really its ends. They are the calisthenics and running and batting practice that, with commitment to teamwork and a deep knowledge of the game, allow one to become a true baseball player. They are the scales and tone practice that form the foundation of professional musicianship.

That is not to say you have to go deeper into the mindful life than the tools I've given you so far will take you. If your main interest now is in meditation exercises and strategies that will help you at home, in the workplace, during a job interview, or while driving or flying or dancing or waiting for the customer service rep to take you off hold, please feel free—and I mean that with great sincerity—to skip now to chapter 18. The more you hone your basic skills and build mental muscle, the better you'll be able to use the more advanced material, whenever and if ever you feel ready or willing to do so. As I have said before, even a single, simple meditation, carefully and diligently practiced over and over until you can instantly apply it during any situation, will build mental muscle and provide you with a stress-busting skill of tremendous power. If that were all the benefit you derived from this book, I would feel honored and pleased.

However, if you'd like to see what the destination looks like while you're still way back on the road, please keep reading through the next chapters. I will warn you that some of the material—on pain and grief, compassion and presence—may be less than pleasant to contemplate as well as difficult to comprehend (I still don't get lots of it, after decades of study). But it's all part of the study of mindfulness, which is the study of a lifetime (or in some people's theological view, the study of many, many, lifetimes).

Summing Up

- Back in chapters 6 and 7, you learned to identify and work with at least one of your dead-end thoughts. You learned to treat a thought as though it were just another kind of object, like a book or sandwich that you could hold or not hold, look at or not look at.

- Thoughts are nothing more than mental objects. Unless they cause a stress reaction, they cannot really affect you. That's why being able to short-circuit stress reactions is so important.

- Identifying and listing difficult thoughts and events that are likely to occur can be useful, because if you know that something may happen and you have prepared a response or action plan, you're better able to deal with it. This is true whether the anticipated item is an event like a flat tire (and you have a jack and spare in your car) or a negative thought (and you're ready to either turn your attention onto your breath, or to use a prepared positive self-talk response, or both).

- You can use the visualization and desensitization skills from chapter 9 to prepare in advance for any negative thought or event on your list. You can do this during any of the multiple short sessions of meditation exercise that you should be continuing to do every single day.

- Sometimes your exercises should be done just to build mental muscle. And sometimes, especially if you have lots of stressful thoughts and events in your life, it's good to use them for desensitization and preparation purposes.

- At the end of this chapter you have a choice. You can continue to work with meditation exercises to use in specific situations (in front of the computer, when on the phone, when bathing or dancing) by skipping to chapter 18. Or you can continue to the next chapter to read about and work with some of the deeper (and sometimes darker) elements of mindfulness, such as compassion, pain, grief, and nonduality. Either choice is fine with me!

13

compassion, pain, and grief

The word "compassion" has its roots in the Latin words *com* ("together") and *pati* ("suffering" or "enduring"). When we experience compassion, we "suffer together" or "feel each other's pain." Thus compassion is quite different from pity, in which "I" feel a sense of sorrow for the tribulations of another creature, human or otherwise ("you" or "it"), who is separate from myself.

When we experience compassion, we understand, on the level of feeling—the "gut level"—that all living creatures experience pain. We see other people as human beings with feelings and an inner life similar to ours—not objects to be manipulated to satisfy ourselves. The theologian Martin Buber calls this sort of relationship an "I-thou" relationship (in contrast to an "I-it" relationship); I will discuss this a bit more in chapter 15.

Compassion is also quite different from the sensation of self-pity, in which we feel sorrow for our own pain: we all know people who are quite capable of feeling sorry for themselves while having little interest in the pain of others.

There are two good reasons to include work on compassion in a mindfulness program. On the level of self-help, it's important to try to identify and then apply compassion (as distinct from self-pity) toward oneself, since so many of us (myself once included) rarely or never experience it. Developing compassion toward oneself helps us to reduce self-judging and negative self-talk behavior, and allows us to console ourselves when dealing with grief or pain. And, as we'll see in chapter 14, when compassion combines with mindfulness, each deepens the other, with a kind of synergy that is unbeatable.

The History of Compassion

The roots of compassion may lie in our evolutionary past, as progressively more complex creatures evolved strategies to help their offspring reach maturity. Some creatures took the sea urchin approach, producing lots of eggs (female sea urchins can release millions at a time) and hoping that some got fertilized and survived without benefit of further parental help. Others, like humans eventually, evolved to produce only a few eggs or offspring, with parents protecting and raising the young. I believe this instinctual tendency toward nurturance and protection has helped to develop in us, as we evolved, a capacity for compassion.

In fact, it appears that we are wired to recognize certain things as being "cute," evoking what we might call a "protective, warm compassion response." Babies or small furry animals with big eyes will produce an "awwww, SO CUTE" reaction in all but the most macho or cynical of us (who probably do experience the response at some level but keep it tightly tamped down because it either does not "fit our image" or leads to painful emotions).

I believe that there is an equal but opposite type of compassion response that could be described as "poignant" or even "heartbreaking," which I'll discuss in the section below on grief. We might call these two variations "loving compassion" and "grieving compassion."

We'll start with an exercise to identify the physiological sensations of "loving compassion."

Exercise 35: Loving Compassion Identification Meditation

1. Spend a moment doing any seated breathing meditation exercise.

2. When you feel relaxed, bring into your mind the memory of a person or a pet you have known and loved. For many of us, it's easier to do this exercise with a beloved pet, perhaps from our childhood, since we are less likely to have mixed feelings about a pet than a person.

3. Visualize that pet (or person), and imagine stroking or hugging them.

4. For many of us, this produces a warm, relaxing feeling. Our shoulders may hang a little looser, and we may sigh. This is a common physical expression of the compassion response.

If you can't evoke a compassion response with this exercise, and you have Internet access, try this (even if it sounds tacky): do a search for "cute kitten" or "cute puppy," whichever you prefer, and look at a few images or video clips to see if you can produce an "awwww" response—a "loving compassion" response.

If you still find it hard to access this physiological response—the warm, loving, relaxed feeling of being with the beloved pet or person—you may want to do one of two things. Since fear and anger are two emotions that block compassion, continue to work with the breath-based meditation exercises, building the mental muscle to short-circuit these emotions. Then, after a few weeks or months, try this exercise again, with whatever image you think may help you to experience a warm and loving or nurturing feeling for a fellow creature. Or you might want to work with some of the additional compassion exercises in Stephen and Ondrea Levine's *Who Dies?* or in my (and my beloved twin sister's) book, *The Three Minute Meditator* (from which the following exercise is adapted).

Exercise 36: Self-Compassion Meditation

If you were successful in identifying the sensation of compassion in the previous exercise, try this one. If not, please return—with gentleness and no judging—to exercise 35 and the instructions that follow it, and try again.

1. Visualize yourself as a young child, perhaps a toddler or preschooler.

2. Imagine yourself holding that child with love and compassion, and without judgment.

3. As you do this, hold your own self now, wrapping your arms around your own body. Imagine that you are that child, still needing love and compassion.

Were you able to elicit the warm, relaxed feeling of the loving compassion response? If not, please work more with exercise 35. (It is, sadly, easier for many of us to feel and show compassion for those other than ourselves.)

An advanced version of this exercise might involve substituting a family member or a friend for yourself in steps 1 through 3.

Begin by choosing someone with whom you don't have too much "negative history"—a favorite relative, perhaps. Eventually, you will find yourself able to do this with a difficult parent or child or other difficult person. However, please remember that allowing yourself to feel compassion for someone does not mean that you make yourself excessively vulnerable to them. Forgiving, in other words, does not mean forgetting.

The more you can cultivate a sense of compassion encompassing both your self and other creatures, the easier it will be—not easy, but easier—to deal with pain of any kind. With compassion, we can deal more mindfully, and more skillfully, with pain—whether mental or physical.

On Pain

Pain is nature's way of telling the organism that something is wrong—if a creature can't feel pain, how does it know something else is chewing on it? So pain is an important part of being alive, and it's unavoidable.

For many of us, physical pain triggers either a flight (fear) response or a fight (anger) response. This often happens so rapidly—we stub the toe, we grit our teeth, we use a four-letter word—that it seems almost a single event. But with practice (in advance of the event), we can learn to short-circuit the response, at least some of the time.

Here's an exercise to help you start practicing this.

Exercise 37: Minor Pain Meditation

1. Think of a situation in which you've experienced a minor and short-lasting physical pain: a stubbed toe, a bumped elbow.

2. Visualize the event, and visualize yourself instantly turning your attention to a simple breath-based meditation for a moment.

3. Do steps 1 and 2 while visualizing a variety of possible minor pain producers, just for half a minute or so each. The practice will help you turn your attention to your breath the next time you have an actual "ouch" experience.

Most people find that if they can focus immediately on the breath, their experience of the pain changes. Due to the breath focus, the mind has no space to tell stories about the pain: "Why did the darn kid leave that toy there?"; "Why can't I be more careful?" Instead the pain is just itself: a short-lived physical sensation. This technique may be termed "breathing into the pain"; when I use it, I sometimes imagine, as I label each in and out, that I can somehow direct my breath into the injured part. The pain remains "just pain," or "just hurting," a physical phenomenon, and does not become "suffering."

Pain versus Suffering

For "suffering" to follow physical pain, it requires the stories of the mind that produce fight-or-flight responses and the anger or fear that follows them. This, unfortunately, means that suffering, in the human creature, does not even require physical pain, but can exist entirely in the mind, most commonly in the "mental discomfort" caused by this process: a thought or "mental story" leads to a fight-or-flight response, which leads to anger or fear.

Fortunately, when we can identify pain—whether from a stubbed toe or a snubbed invitation—and use a breath-based meditation quickly enough to short-circuit the attendant fight-or-flight response, we can begin to change the way we relate to pain, to our great benefit.

Please repeat exercise 37 now, but this time, instead of a minor physical pain producer, replace the first step with a minor mental pain producer: a slightly annoying thought or situation (the friend late for lunch, the errand you don't really want to do) that produces a slightly negative mental story.

We can also use the sense of loving self-compassion from exercise 36 (once we have identified it and can summon it—at least sometimes—at will) to relieve suffering. To create a more advanced version of exercise 37, we add a step after step 2, in which we insert a moment of self-compassion. So we breathe into the pain—physical or mental—then we feel compassion for ourselves, the one in pain. This technique may also help you to work with other exercises that may cause mental pain to arise, such as identifying self-judging tendencies or the difficult thoughts and situations that are likely to "hit our fan" (as we do in chapter 12).

When we are experiencing pain (physical or mental), but can keep most of our mental attention on our breath to short-circuit stress responses, and also summon a sense of compassion for ourselves as "the one who is in pain," we can reduce suffering. This is an extremely difficult practice, but it begins simply: by starting to practice it on the small pains of daily life, starting now.

Compassion and Self-Soothing

Self-soothing is a way of trying to deal with pain or fear, and sometimes with anger. Some self-soothing behaviors—like those utilizing drugs, alcohol, or extreme levels of exercise, diet, or obsessive focus on a particular sports team or hobby—might be considered to be more forms of self-medication than of self-soothing. Chapter 20 is devoted to the subject of self-soothing; I will just mention now that developing a sense of compassion will be of key importance to dealing skillfully with self-soothing behavior, whether positive or negative.

On Grief

My basic definition of grief is this: grief is the pain and suffering we feel at the loss of something or someone we value or love. This is an accurate definition; still, its simplicity belies the depth and complexity of the subject.

Many years ago, when I had first begun to work with the concept of dead-end thoughts, a student asked me an important question: "Is grief a dead-end thought?" The answer to that question is, "it depends"—depends, that is, on the cause and the form of the grief. For example, sometimes what we call grief (as in "He is grieving the loss of his job") may be more akin to a complex stress response, composed of fear at the prospect of not having a job, and anger at the job's loss and the attendant loss of face that job loss can entail in our culture. In this case, allowing these emotions—however unavoidable, natural, and valid for some length of time—to control or overwhelm us for too long could impair our ability to move on. Even in the case of the death of a loved one, feelings of anger and fear may exacerbate and extend the true grief that is just sadness for loss, so that eventually bringing those other emotions into the light of day with great patience and compassion can be skillful.

I believe that grief is also cumulative. By this I mean that, often, what might seem a "small" loss can cause a grief that some might consider disproportionate. But the grief we feel at a seemingly smaller loss can revive the grief we've felt at all the losses in our life, some of which we may not have mourned in a way that allows closure—that is, a mindful, slow diminishment of strong grief over time, and an eventual return to regular life.

Working with Grief

I'm no expert in grief work, and the subject deserves its own book, or shelf of books, rather than a few paragraphs. But from my work with hospice, from my study of the work of great teachers like Stephen and Ondrea Levine, and from creating five-day workshops such as "Zen and the Art of Harmonica:™ Playing with Life, Death, Grief, Loss, Zest, and the Whole Nine Yards," I have developed strategies for helping people to work with deep and intense emotional responses to painful and difficult situations.

I have found that a combination of breathing meditations to reduce stress responses, compassion meditations to deal with the sadness of loss, mindful attention to whatever thoughts arise, and lots of patience can help us "get over" the grief. The support of friends and a skilled therapist with experience in grief counseling is also invaluable, as is hospice when we are dealing with terminal illness.

Briefly, when working with grief, alternating between allowing oneself to experience "just grieving" and breathing-based meditation exercises to help "keep the mind out of the process" for a moment can be very useful. At the very least, it provides a short respite from the pain of grieving. It can also be helpful, in later stages of grieving, to try to understand and feel the universal nature of grief and loss.

As with loving compassion, I believe that most of us are wired so that we recognize certain images (in real life, or as thoughts) as "poignant" or even "heartbreaking" (evoking a sad, empathetic compassion response, a "grieving compassion"). An image of the Pietà—the classic Christian artistic representation of Jesus' mother Mary holding the body of her dead son—will produce in most of us a sigh and a sorrowful, "heartache" sensation, regardless of our religious affiliations or lack thereof. Developing this sense of "grieving compassion," and the realization that all who live suffer grief, can help us to deal with this most painful of human emotions.

Again I will mention Stephen and Ondrea Levine's book *Who Dies?* as a resource: I believe it is the best book available on the subject of grief and suffering.

Practice Imperfect

Sometimes bad stuff happens and we don't handle it very skillfully. Not too long ago, I had to spend an unpleasant night at the airport in Washington, D.C., when I'd expected to sleep that night in my own bed at home in Vermont. It was partly my own fault for scheduling a late flight home, so I felt grumpy about that, and I was tired after a set of presentations. "Meditation," I thought. "Baloney. I'm mad!" But I knew that's just what would help me get through the night.

When something of this magnitude happens—deeply irritating and of some duration, but not life-threatening—I try to divide my attention. And not between my breath and the situation, but at a deeper level.

That night, I split my attention amongst: 1) feeling angry at the airline; 2) feeling angry at myself for bad scheduling and for creating a job that requires air travel; 3) feeling angry at the weather; and 4) my meditation practice. I meditated for a while. Then I got mad for a while. Then I realized that I'd been grumping and complaining, and returned to the meditation. (This last is analogous to losing track of my count in a breathing and counting meditation, noticing it, and returning to the breathing and counting—it's really the same process, just at a higher level.)

When I miss the flight (and use a few choice words), I might allow myself to get angry at myself for not practicing what I preach, for being an imperfect meditator and an imperfect human being. But this does nothing useful. I'd be practicing self-hatred, wasting time better spent turning to a moment of breath and then compassion meditation.

Summing Up

- Cultivating compassion is essential to a real mindfulness practice. It connects us with other people and helps us deal with pain and grief in such a way as to reduce suffering.

- The exercises in this chapter will help you get in touch with the loving compassion response—the feelings and sensations you get when you are feeling connected empathically to another creature—and begin cultivating a sense of compassion for yourself. Try them when you feel ready.

- Pain can be either physical or mental in origin. Rehearsing a practice of "breathing into" instances of minor physical and mental pain can help you build the capacity to do so should more severe episodes of pain come upon you.

- Grief is among the most difficult of human emotions. Practicing patience and self-compassion, and getting help from others, will alleviate it over time. So will reducing the number of stress responses triggered by thoughts associated with grief. Mindfulness offers true solace in a way that medicine, distractions, or other temporary measures cannot.

- Meditating is always hardest to do when you need it the most. But being angry at yourself for not meditating successfully is paradoxical and not useful. Smile compassionately to yourself when it happens, then instantly refocus your attention onto your breath.

being present

"David Harp!" the teacher calls out. "Present!" I reply. What does this exchange mean? Well, in this context, "present" means "David is in the classroom, and conscious enough to hear his name and respond as he's expected to." But there's much more to "being present" than that. It's an abstract concept; if you like, skip this chapter for a week or a month or a year, and spend your time profitably in building mental muscle. When you need a new challenge, come back to this page.

Being Present, Being Mindful, and "Living in the Now"

"Being present" can be used synonymously with "being mindful." Another term (which my coauthor and I use extensively in *The Three Minute Meditator*) is "living in the now." Many of us spend a lot of our mental time with our attention focused on the past, in the form of memories (both pleasant and unpleasant). Thinking of those past events in the present brings the past into our present. Memories about things that were pleasant become desires that we think about now, and that can launch us into plans for the future ("I really enjoyed that trip to the Florida Keys two years ago—I wish I were there now—better start looking at flights and hotels online"). Memories about things that were unpleasant take the form of fears that we allow to stress us now and that we worry about for the future ("The last party at Shaneen's house was awful; no one talked to me. I just can't go—but how can I get out of it? She's my boss.").

Sometimes we spend mental time in the future without the use of memory. We plan, we attempt to predict, and, naturally, we worry. Sometimes we get angry because of our predictions ("If he says that to me, I'll just blow my stack!"). Our fears or angers about the future affect us in the present, since they trigger stress responses.

Just Looking, Just Listening, Just Being

We can short-circuit those past-caused and future-caused stress responses just as we've been doing with any type of stress response—by focusing on the breath with a meditation exercise. However, we create a deeper level of mindfulness when we avoid certain types of thoughts entirely for a while, by using the "just looking" exercise 21, or the "just listening" exercise 22 (both in chapter 8) and reading the "just doing" section of that chapter. During this type of meditation, we are trying to avoid all mental processes not related to the physical aspects of what we are doing. When I practice these exercises, for a moment, instead of being "David listening" or "David looking," it feels almost as though "just listening" or "just looking" is all that is happening, with the "David" part somewhere in the background, ignored for the moment.

This brief disappearance of the self is a glimpse into the concept in metaphysics known as "Advaita" or "nonduality." In experiencing nonduality, the meditation practitioner reduces his or her identity with both the body and the mind, in favor of identification with the universe as a whole: the philosophy of Advaita holds that this is the self's true and natural state. Some of my students and I do meditation exercises (briefly described in the next chapter) to work toward attempting to attain the barest hint of a whisper of a taste of this state. Experiencing it—however briefly—is considered by many experts on mindfulness to be the most advanced realization of mindfulness practice, if rarely achieved.

The Unbeatable Combination: Mindfulness and Compassion

This last statement may be true, but, in my opinion, the use of mindfulness tools and techniques to short-circuit stress responses and to cultivate compassion are utterly worthwhile in themselves and, taken together, are powerful tools for living.

When we develop awareness of the fears and angers of our own minds and can control our responses to them, and when we develop a deep sense of compassion for ourselves and others, we can live more in the present than in the past or future. And these two goals, awareness and compassion, are mutually reinforcing. As we become more compassionate, it is easier to explore our own minds without fear, anger, denial, or resistance. As we become more deeply aware by exploring our minds, we find it easier to become more compassionate. As in an arch made of two curved stones, each supports the other as it rises to the heavens.

Summing Up

- "Being present" means not allowing thoughts about our past (memories) or future (fears, plans, antici-pated pleasures) to affect our present. If we notice this happening to us to an excessive degree—that is, one that affects our ability to enjoy or function in the present, or occupies a lot of our attention—refocusing onto the breath brings us back into the present.

- We can also stay present by practicing the "just doing" exercises of chapter 8, such as the "just looking" exercise 21 or "just listening" exercise 22. With practice, these exercises can "take the 'you' out of the equation": not "David doing," but "just doing."

- The "just doing" exercises can give us a glimpse of the extremely rare state of nondualistic mindfulness, in which we feel identified with the entire universe rather than with our individual body or mind.

- Exalted though that state might be, simply develop-ing awareness and compassion form an unbeatable combination, which takes on a life of its own: being more aware makes it easier to be more compassion-ate, and being more compassionate makes it easier to be more aware. The benefits of this are immense—with or without an awareness of nonduality!

15

on nonduality and
spirituality

Even though you may not believe in a deity of any sort, or subscribe to a particular religion, or believe in any form of continued existence after the death of the body, I suspect that anyone reading a book of this type is interested in the question of how to "lead a good life." This is arguably the ultimate question of any philosophical, metaphysical, or theological system of thought. If these sorts of explorations interest you, you may find the concept of nonduality to be of some interest. (If not, please feel free skip this chapter.) A full exploration of this concept is beyond the scope of this book, but I'll attempt to give you a little taste in this chapter.

Nonduality

As we discussed in an earlier chapter, with the development of compassion we recognize that every other living person is a "subject," with an internal life similar in general, if not in the specifics, to our own—complex, inconsistent, and often pain-filled. At this compassionate level of mindfulness, we see the world as filled with subjects—individuals, each as valid and worthy of existence, and facing the same issues and struggles, as we are. A nondualistic level of mindfulness takes this awareness a step higher.

Nonduality, or "Advaita"—from the Sanskrit *a* ("not") and *dvaita* ("dual, two, dualism")—is the goal of a superadvanced state of total mindfulness, in which one does not feel separate in any way from the entire universe.

So if the state of compassion eliminates the division between one subject (you) and another subject (me), the experience of nondualism eliminates the very concept of subjects, since there is only one—what some nondeistic theologians call the "all-that-is" and others call "the underlying ground of being." A more traditionally minded nondualist theologian would use the term

"God," and say that we are all part of that being, and insepa-rable from it.

A standard method of training advanced yoga or mindful-ness students in nondualistic consciousness is to have them ponder and focus attention on the sensation of "I am" or "con-scious presence." When we are in the midst of a "just doing" meditation, there may be no sensation of "I" at all—there is "just doing." Once you are able to reach this state of "just doing," investigate the state of "am-ness." Who is looking? Who is lis-tening? I am. Who is I? Am I the body? Am I my brain? My mind? If my mind is quiet, is there simply some kind of...sense of being present...that is looking or listening? These are the questions that the teachers of Advaita ask us to ask.

On Prayer

Fortunately, even without an experience of nondualism, mind-fulness has great spiritual benefits—whatever your religion or belief system.

If prayer is part of our spiritual life, for example, more focused attention and relief from anger and fear can only help any connection that we might seek with the divine. If we have practiced "just looking," "just listening," and "just doing," we will be ready to practice "just praying."

To see how this works, you might—like the islanders in chapter 5—use a very brief prayer from your own tradition in a simple step-counting meditation, saying a syllable each time you take a step; or in a breathing meditation, focusing on the prayer on each exhale or inhale. In the Christian tradition, you might use the Jesus prayer, which in its simplest form can be "Lord have mercy" (*Kyrie eleison*, in Greek). No matter what faith you practice, any short, memorized prayer can be used in this way, to combine prayer with meditation.

Summing Up

- We can use the "just doing" exercises to investigate the state of nondualism, by asking ourselves questions such as "Who is doing the 'just looking' or the 'just listening'?" when our mind is quiet.

- Any short, memorized prayer can be combined with either a walking or a breathing meditation. This increases mental focus while decreasing distracting emotions like anger and fear. "Staying present" while praying can change a rote experience into a much more meaningful one: "Just Praying."

- The Nisargadatta and Frydman book in the "Resources" section and Levine's *Who Dies?* are my favorite books on this topic.

16

building a mindfulness strategy

When I initially conceptualized this book, I thought of having separate chapters on applying the mindfulness techniques at work, at home, while traveling, and in "waiting" situations. But as I wrote, it became clear that this would create artificial distinctions, since many of the events we encounter in all those environments have elements in common. We have to wait for the printer to print at work, wait on line at the airline counter, wait for our children or our friends to arrive at the restaurant. Difficult interpersonal circumstances occur at home, in the office, at the dentist's.

In both these kinds of situations—waiting for something to occur, and experiencing interpersonal stress—and in many others, the meditations that will help have very similar steps. Thus it makes sense to review and discuss what we might call the strategic plan of a mindfulness practice.

Then we'll start identifying some of the negative self-talk that arises in different environments, and finding opportunities to use meditation exercises in specific situations. If you've been trying each meditation exercise as you encounter it, and using your favorites to build mental muscle in tiny increments throughout the day, you'll be able to use the following chapters to be more mindful at work, at home, and on the road, whether you're performing a task or waiting for something to happen.

I'll end the book with a section on the behaviors that we use to soothe ourselves, from eating to watching TV to sports, with some suggestions on using mindfulness to enhance the benefits of our self-soothing acts and reduce their negative impacts.

The Mindfulness Strategy

I believe there are four main steps to building a mindfulness practice (three of which you've already tried, and one you may not have), with one final extra step that is worth working toward but exquisitely difficult to achieve. You already know the first three, but a review may be helpful.

Step One: Build Mental Muscle

We begin by learning at least a few basic meditation exercises involving focus on the breath, and by creating enough opportunities to practice them in short increments so that we can eventually:

- short-circuit any stress response at will (remember that a stress response means any fight-or-flight response that is not needed to preserve life and limb, or is otherwise un-useful);

- be able to stay totally focused on any task without allowing our mind to tell us distracting stories (as we learned to do in the "just looking" and "just listening" exercises, allowing us to cultivate the state of "just doing").

Step Two: Rehearse, Visualize, and Desensitize

Unless and until mindfulness has become so much a part of your life that you can use its tools and techniques in any situation, and you have gained the ability to "just do" any type of task with complete focus, it will be necessary for you to rehearse and visualize using these tools in advance, in preparation for difficult situations. Start with the dead-end-thought split attention/ desensitization meditation (exercise 19, in chapter 7). As this exercise becomes easier, work with the anticipated event desensitization meditations (exercise 26) to help prepare yourself to deal mindfully with difficult situations as they happen.

Step Three: See It Coming Before It Hits the Fan

In chapter 12, you learned how to treat your thoughts as objects like any other objects, and to examine and name your thoughts as they arose, concentrating especially on negative thoughts and the events that tend to trigger them. By investigating your thoughts in this way, you can become aware of potentially difficult events or thoughts in advance. You can then practice using your mindfulness tools on them, as in practice step 2.

Step Four: Cultivate Compassion

Being alive and aware is not easy. The first three steps will help you avoid unnecessary suffering, but you will still experience pain, loss, and grief. If you work to develop your sense of compassion, using the exercises in chapter 13, you will have a superlative tool to apply when life is hard, or when things go badly. Like many people, you may not decide to do this step until you are in pain. That's okay. Your capacity for compassion is always there, and sometimes it's easier to motivate ourselves to develop it when we are forced to, by pain.

Step Five (for Saints and Sages Only): Wrestle with Nonduality and the Existential Dilemma

The more we can feel a part of something bigger than ourselves—something bigger even than the whole world that we inhabit—the less separateness and loss we feel. In Hindu metaphysics, the unity of the universe is called Advaita, or nonduality, and many meditation practitioners of all kinds believe that experiencing that unity—however briefly—is the ultimate goal of a mindful life. Only the greatest saints and sages experience this unity to any great degree during their lifetimes, but you may find the pursuit worth your time. It may be the only way, outside of a religious belief in life after death, to overcome what philosophers call the "existential dilemma"—which is the consciousness that we are alive and that we will die. Chapter 15 contains a brief introduction to nonduality, and a few reading suggestions to feed your understanding of this important concept.

Summing Up

- What we might call the "Strategic Plan" of a mindfulness practice has four main steps, and one advanced one.

- These steps are: Building Mental Muscle, Rehearsing/ Visualizing/Desensitizing, Learning How to See It Coming Before It Hits the Fan, Cultivating Compassion, and (for Saints and Sages Only) Wrestling with Nonduality and the Existential Dilemma.

17

interpersonal mindfulness at home and work

Mindfulness can have strong, positive effects on the way you feel and behave at home and in the workplace. You don't need to learn any new meditation exercises to start improving your interactions with other people—you've already tried plenty! All you need are one or two favorites that are easy to stay focused on and to use, and the ability to identify the ways and situations in which you can apply them when needed.

You may feel very busy right now—too "busy" to be mindful; many people feel this way. If so, try this: replace "busy" with the word "active" in this particular piece of self-talk. Why? The word "busy" implies a focus on specific tasks (such as those pertaining to one's "business"), and it can connote a burdensome load of work to be done. But the word "active" connotes capableness and a zest for accomplishing things; "active" has room for many types of activities—and mindfulness is a type of activity.

Between You and Me: The Art of Mindful Conversation

When in conversation, we can use mindfulness on a number of levels. We can split our attention to notice the play of our own thoughts as we listen to what the other person is saying: are we simply perceiving the sound of their words; looking for the hidden message behind those words; or planning our own reply rather than paying attention to what they are saying? More importantly, during heated, contentious, or other difficult interactions, we can divide our attention between a breathing focus (defusing our fight-or-flight response and decreasing the attendant anger or fear) and the content of the conversation. Doing so will allow us to seek resolution based on the reality of the situation rather than on fear or anger (and we'll be building mental muscle all the while).

How Much Do You "Need" to Hear?

In chapter 8, you began to practice a simulated form of interpersonal interaction: the annoying-personality split attention meditation (exercise 24). In it, you practiced splitting your attention between a focus on one of your breathing meditations and a focus on a TV or radio personality you dislike.

If you've practiced that exercise, you'll find it only slightly more difficult to split your attention between a conversation with a real, live person and your breathing meditation. If you do find it difficult to split and balance your focus successfully, try this:

- When you don't really need to pay much attention to the content of what's being said, use a breath label and count up to four breaths: "in…one, out…one, in…two, out…two."

- When it's important that you process and remember the content of the conversation, use a simpler breath-labeling meditation: "iiinnn, oouutttt"; this type of meditation is easy to drop and pick up, drop and pick up on a second-by-second basis as you need to pay more or less attention to the conversation.

Start Simply

Begin practicing this technique during low-stress, casual conversations. It will be easier in a small group than one on one, since your level of verbal participation will go way down when your attention is split. In fact, most people (myself included) need to relinquish most of their breath attention to say anything more complex than a short, standard phrase like "That's right" or "Uh-huh" or "Wow."

If others notice that you're not saying much ("You're so quiet today, Dave..."), a great response is "I'm just listening." This is something most people are happy to hear—we all want to feel "listened to." (It's also a pun, since you are practicing "just listening," right?) Follow the conversation with your eyes, looking at or toward whoever's speaking, so that you look fully involved. If being quiet makes you uncomfortable, that's just another thing to be mindful about, another piece of information about yourself to explore. Where did that one come from?

You can also be mindful about any specific comment you feel compelled to insert into the conversation. Before speaking, mentally (and mindfully) ask yourself, "Is this useful? Is there some reason I want to say it? Should I think about it more before saying it?" This is another element of mindful speech that is best to begin practicing in casual conversation, where the stakes are pretty low.

Mindful Listening and Speaking: Higher Stakes

When you've done some low-stakes practice, kick it up a notch by using the same exact techniques during interactions with people who you find mildly difficult, whether relatives, colleagues, clients, or patients. You'll probably find that your stress response is more likely to be triggered than it is during casual conversation. So you'll need to be more aware of the early stirrings and symptoms of the fight-or-flight response, and constantly ready to shift more of your attention onto your breathing meditation. In this situation, should you miss something that is said while you're focusing on the breath, be prepared to insert this useful statement: "Could you please repeat what you just said? I want to make sure I really understand what you mean." Most people will be glad to do this, since it makes it appear that you really want to hear what they are saying. And you do, but on your own (mindful) terms!

After practicing in low-stakes conversations, and in conversations with people you find mildly irritating or difficult, you can begin to apply mindfulness techniques to more important or stressful interactions. To do this, you'll have to use everything you've learned so far, as discussed in the following example.

Mindful Communication: A Workplace Example

Consider the act of walking from your workstation to your boss's office for a meeting that's going to be stressful. If you knew the meeting was coming, perhaps you've already done some desensitization work by visualizing the interaction. Normally (in a nonmindful state) as you walk down the hall, your mind would be filled with thoughts about what you're going to say to her, and what she may say back to you, and how you'll feel—glad or mad, relieved or disappointed—about her words. But now, you use the mental muscle you've gained to keep your attention completely focused on the sensations of each foot hitting the floor and of your breathing as you walk. Nonmindful walking time would probably be occupied by either a stress response or a pleasurable fantasy of dubious likelihood, neither of which will be useful during the actual meeting. The mindful preparation and calming, in-the-moment focus will help you to arrive at her office in a relaxed and mindful mood.

As you listen, you split your attention between your breath and her words. In a high-stakes case like this, you'd probably use the simplest breath labeling meditation ("iiinnn...ooutttt") as she speaks. If the content of the conversation is complex (figures or statistics that you need to listen to, names you need to remember), drop the breath focus as needed and focus on the words. But as soon as you feel stressed, do another few seconds of breath focus. If you've practiced doing this in lower-stakes conversations, and done the mindfulness exercise with the annoying TV or radio host (exercise 24), it will be easier to use your skills in this more difficult situation. You will emerge from the interaction—whatever its content—calmer and more collected than you might have otherwise.

Mindful Communication at Home

The big difference between communication at home and communication at work is that you're probably not related to the people at work by ties of blood or marriage (unless you work for a family business). Communications with children, old friends, or parents are very likely to be affected by a long mutual history. This means you'll have to do some "how to see it coming" work (see chapter 12) to prepare you to be mindful during the actual communication. Preparing for a day at the beach with both your children and your aging parents? You'll need to do:

- some "how to see it coming" identification of problem thoughts or events that are likely to arise;

- some visualization and desensitization exercise around those areas, so that you'll have a higher likelihood of applying mindfulness techniques (such as split attention) when those thoughts or events arise.

While you're at the beach (or on the road there and back), you'll need to be alert to stress responses as they arise, and prepared to switch to a simple breath-focused meditation as soon as you start feeling the symptoms of stress.

What Happens When You Mess Up?

No one—at least no one I've ever met—is perfectly mindful all the time. You have to *expect* to blow it, at least sometimes. And it's helpful to be prepared to deal with the situation when you do. Here's a general strategy for that.

1. Try to see it coming: realize that it's not only possible, but likely that in some situations your mindfulness skills will be inadequate to the task. You may want to consciously practice in advance, with visualization, steps 2 through 4, below.

2. Be ready, if you do "blow it," to notice that you've lost your focus on the breath or other short-circuiting strategy, and acted unskillfully, as soon as you can. Doing this promptly means you'll be acting badly for as short a time as possible.

3. Instantly return your attention to the breath, to short-circuit the current crisis.

4. It may then be appropriate to apologize—"I'm really sorry, I lost it for a minute there." You will have to judge whether it's the right time for an apology.

Rehearsing this entire process, with visualization, may help you to deal with such situations. Adding, after step 3, a moment of compassion for those affected by your lack of mindfulness and for yourself will help also. Working with a compassion exercise (exercise 35) will help you be able to be compassionate.

On the Telephone

Everything I've just said about mindful communication in person also applies when you're using the phone—except that the phone is easier, in some ways, since you don't have to appear to be focused entirely on the speaker, who can't see you. But it goes both ways: since you can't see the other person, you'll need to pay more attention to her tone so as to understand her emotional state (if that is important to the content of the call, or to your response).

I try to do a very short telephone mindfulness exercise before dealing with an incoming call. If I'm answering the phone myself, I allow it to ring three times before I pick it up. During those three rings, I do a very short breath-labeling meditation, combined with a mindful acknowledgement that this call could have very good news, very bad news, or neither, and that I have no control over this. After I exhale, I pick up the handset: "Hello. David Harp." Or if someone else has answered the phone and I'm informed that the call is for me, I tell whoever answered, "I'll be on the line in a minute." Then I do the same as when picking up the phone myself.

This exercise is a great mental muscle builder and a great reminder that we have little real control over the world we live in. And it prepares me to handle the call in the most mindful way possible, whether the person on the other end is a telemarketer, my best friend, or a potential client.

Summing Up

- Interactions with other people are an important area in which to practice mindfulness. You can begin doing so with the exercises you have already learned and practiced.

- If interpersonal situations tend to be stressful for you, practice exercise 24 (the annoying-personality split attention exercise in chapter 8). Practice it a lot.

- Use the "how to see it coming" techniques in chapter 12 to identify, in advance, interpersonal situations that will stress you. Then rehearse for these situations by visualizing them in advance.

- You will "blow it" sometimes. Have a fallback strategy for when you do, as follows: notice that you've blown it as quickly as possible; return your attention to your breath for a moment; then apologize as appropriate. Compassion—for those affected by you, and yourself—will help. Please work with exercise 35 so that you'll be able to apply it when you need it.

18

mindfulness on the road, and on the fly

Traveling can be a joy or a torture. Either way, there are good opportunities for mindfulness on the road—Jack Kerouac's characters may not have taken advantage of them, but you can. Here are some ways to start.

Drive Yourself Sane

If the idea of a "driving meditation" conjures up images of zoning out, eyes closed, on a deep "ommm" mantra while whipping down the highway at seventy miles an hour, you're in for a surprise. During the beginning levels of driving meditation, your entire mental focus will be on the perceptual components of... safe driving. The following exercise will help you build mental muscle, which will soon enable you to safely add a breathing exercise component—and yet more mental muscle building—to your drive time.

Safety notes:

1. If you are a new driver or are prone to accidents or inattention, or if you are taking any medications or have any physical or emotional condition that might affect your driving safety, DO NOT use this exercise—even though it is designed to make your driving safer. Wait until you've been using the other meditation exercises for a few years, then review the instructions and, if appropriate, discuss them with your health care providers before trying the exercise.

2. Any time you are doing any driving meditation, know without a doubt that the safety of your driving is your first and foremost consideration. Never do any of these exercises when the driving or road conditions are congested or challenging in any way.

Exercise 38: Super Safe Driving Meditation

Imagine being a driver in a NASCAR or Grand Prix race. Would you allow thoughts about your gracious victory speech to enter your mind as you raced, or speculations about whether your ex-wife is watching? Of course not! Even a fraction of a second of inattention to car and track could mean not just the loss of the race, but the loss of your life.

This exercise is a way of practicing that level of attention in your own car. Do this exercise while driving during good weather on a familiar stretch of road: a limited access highway is probably safest. Your goal throughout the exercise is to keep your attention entirely focused on your driving.

1. Focus your sight only on the road in front of you, with occasional and swift glances at the rearview mirror and the speedometer as needed. Notice the position of cars around you, and any place where a car, animal, bicycle, or pedestrian might enter the roadway.

2. Attune your hearing only to horns, sirens, or other important driving sounds. No radio. No conversation with passengers, if there are any (try this the first few times when driving alone; then later on, if you have passengers, tell them in advance that you won't be talking for a while).

3. When you notice any thought not related to safe driving, use your mental muscle to bring your attention immediately back to your driving. Pretend that it's

a matter of life and death—and of course, it really is. We just don't often remember to think of it that way.

Exercise 39: Safe Driving and Thought-Naming Meditation

When you feel completely comfortable with the above exercise and have spent some time with it, add one new part. If you have been working on thought-naming (exercise 34, in chapter 12), incorporate that technique into your safe-driving meditation. Should a non-driving-related thought arise, label it with a name that you have already come up with when listing your problem thoughts (chapter 12)—or a new name—then instantly return your full attention to your driving. If you can't *immediately* come up with a new or existing name, just return to your driving.

Safe Driving and Breathing Meditations

If you've spent a *minimum* of a few months doing breathing meditation exercises without driving, you can add a breathing component to your safe driving meditation. Begin by labeling your inhales and exhales—"iiinnnn…oouuttt…"—as you drive, with only as much mental attention focused on your breathing as is necessary to determine whether you are inhaling or exhaling. Should any circumstance require your full attention (needing to pass someone or slow down; a potential obstacle in the road; and so on), lose the breath focus, instantly!

Driving on the highway, for me, is a great time to build mental muscle. Instead of listening to talk radio or classic rock, or obsessing over some real or imagined incident, or (this is bad!) talking on my cell phone in states where it is still legal (which it probably shouldn't be), I do simple breath-based meditation exercises. Sometimes I'll count my breaths up to four, over and over. Sometimes I'll decide to count my breaths "from here until I get to Brattleboro," for example.

Since I like to drive with both hands on the steering wheel, I sometimes do a right hand, left hand breathing meditation (exercise 23, in chapter 8) while driving. I allow my left hand to grasp the wheel a bit more tightly than my right as I inhale, and as I switch to the exhale, I tighten my right-hand grip a bit while relaxing my left a little.

Road Rage

If you suffer from road rage, you should probably be on the bus (in which case you'll need to turn to the section on commuting, below). But if you occasionally find yourself annoyed at another driver or at bad traffic conditions, you can use a breathing meditation to help short-circuit that fight response, as long as it's safe to do so. Sometimes it's best to pull off the road and do just one minute of meditation, since driving when angry is not safe either.

Do you have an automotive pet peeve, such as people who wait until the last minute to merge when a lane is closed? If so, as soon as you see that "Right lane closed 1 mile" sign, use the above exercises to keep your attention on your driving and your breath, and off those annoying lane cutters! You'll reduce stress and build mental muscle.

I believe that driving mindfully as I describe it puts you more in the company of the great racing drivers than in the company of those who talk while looking at passengers; phone or even text while driving; fiddle with the radio endlessly; or allow anger or anxiety, daydreams or distracting thoughts to affect their driving.

Mindfulness on the Fly

Since I don't recommend that on-duty airline pilots meditate (although it might, indeed, improve their flying if done carefully and mindfully), for most of us it's pretty easy to meditate while we travel by air and navigate airports:

- If you're fearful about flying but have to do it anyway, use your breath meditations as you would to short-circuit any stress response.

- If you're not generally afraid of flying, but turbulence arises or bad weather makes a take-off or landing problematic, do the same thing.

- As you travel through the airport, whether rushing to catch your plane or shuffling shoeless to the security counter, do a walking (or jogging) meditation. Since you already know your gate number, what could be more useful to think of?

- If you're worried about making a connection, or about a flight being cancelled, do what is necessary (get to the gate; get on line at the customer service counter), then meditate. Watch as your stress response begins to trigger each time an announcement begins, and turn half of your attention onto your breathing.

- If angry feelings come up when your flight is cancelled or when you have to wait for an extra hour on the tarmac, try to remember that you have something extremely valuable on which to spend your time—developing your mindfulness practice.

Opportunities abound to practice meditation while waiting in airports, but I'll cover more "waiting" meditations in the next chapter. So for now, I'll simply suggest that—in addition to using meditation to deal with fear or anger, as described above—you spend a few moments when airborne contemplating what an unusual situation you are in, thousands of feet above the ground and moving at a speed of hundreds of miles per hour. Consider the environmental costs of flying as well as its testament to human ingenuity. Should these reflections bring up any feelings (or other thoughts), experience them without self-judgment, splitting your attention between them and your breath.

Commuting

Since commuting when you're the driver just counts as driving, this section is more about ride-sharing or using public transportation.

In either case, you will find yourself in an interpersonal situation, stuffed into a car or van, bus or train with a group of people whom you may or may not like or know all that well (if at all).

In this situation, instead of reading or turning up the volume on your music player, you can use the group interaction as an opportunity to do some mindfulness practice. In a ride-share, especially, you can use your fellow passengers' conversation to do an annoying-personality split attention meditation (exercise 24, in chapter 8), or try some of the interpersonal mindfulness work from chapter 17. Practice a like, dislike, neutral: judging meditation (exercise 32) using the group's chatter as your object of attention, then switch to a judging/nonjudging meditation (exercise 33) with an auditory rather than visual focus. You can have a bit of fun and build mental muscle, however you feel about your fellow riders. On public transit, you can often use these exercises as well, or work on any of a number of other meditations, using breathing, visualizations, thought-naming, and even compassion.

Summing Up

- If you are a good, competent, confident driver, driving offers excellent opportunities for mental muscle building—as long as you understand that the driving *always* comes first!

- Forget about doing driving meditation exercises if you are not a good, experienced, unimpaired driver traveling in good conditions.

- Flying and commuting offer great opportunities to become anxious or annoyed, and are thus ideal environments for working on a mindfulness practice. When you can take a trying environment and use it for the most positive endeavor possible, that's mindfulness!

wait a minute: mindfulness without motion

Waiting—when all motion comes to a stop—provides us with a convenient time to practice mindfulness. We might use the time to do a simple mental muscle–building exercise, such as a breath-focus meditation. Or we might, at a slightly more advanced level, use an enforced lack of motion—whether waiting in a traffic jam or in the doctor's office—to examine our emotional state in a mindful way, as an exercise in developing self-knowledge.

We can often insert a very short mindfulness exercise into a portion of a task that might otherwise require most of our mental attention. While on the checkout line in a store, while the next program is opening on the computer, while walking to the printer to pick up our newest pages—these can all be converted into opportunities for mindfulness practice, instead of being simply mindless but necessary tasks.

In Front of the Computer

In the tiny moments while your screen is refreshing or the document is being emailed, turn your attention to your breath. Notice whether you are inhaling or exhaling, and start to label your breath. It may be hard to believe, but even noticing the last half of an exhale, and mentally saying "oouutt" as you finish it, builds mental muscle. The ability to insert a second of mindfulness into any situation is nothing to disparage!

When things aren't going quite smoothly—when your computer is tormenting you to some degree, whether with new software you have not quite mastered, a slow Internet connection, or a possible hard drive meltdown, a stress response is likely. Even before you call for help, short-circuit the stress response with a breath-based meditation exercise.

At the Airport

Since 9/11, flying commercially has become more stressful for us all, with more line-waiting and cancelled flights and congested airports. But airport waiting, unpleasant though it is, provides us with lots of mindfulness opportunities amid all the boredom, anger, or anxiety. You can also, if you've cultivated the necessary mental muscle, use these opportunities to practice mindfulness in of all sorts of ways: breath-focus meditations; step-counting or labeling meditations; visualization and desensitization meditations; whatever you feel moved to work on while you're stalled.

On Line and On Hold

This one's a no-brainer. When the line is moving swiftly enough so that you can at least shuffle, do a very slow walking and breathing exercise. If you're barely moving, do some breath counting or labeling, or some "just looking" and "just listening" work (since you are likely in a public place if you're on a line). Compassion practice using nearby strangers as objects of focus—or yourself—is another good way to use this time.

Call that 800 number, and what often happens? You're put on hold for some impossible-to-determine period. You can gripe, you can read, you can peruse the Internet, or you can throw in at least a minute or two of meditation practice. It's your call!

Waiting for Others

Waiting for someone else can be hard, especially if you have a shared history—and even more so if your shared history involves lots of you waiting for that person. The more skillfully you can use the time waiting, the more useful that wait becomes. Imagine the late arrival's surprise when he rushes up, expecting your wrath, and you say, "Oh, I didn't mind. I was meditating."

Summing Up

Periods of down time or waiting—even tiny, seconds-long scraps of time—are perfect opportunities to practice mindfulness. Taking these opportunities as they come builds mental muscle and mindfulness, whether you are practicing focus on the breath, observing the negative thoughts provoked by the wait, or musing mindfully on the uncertainty of the human condition.

20

soothing the self

When creatures are in pain, they need to be soothed. Since pain is a part of life, so must soothing be. Many of us seek to be soothed by others—a parent when we are young, friends or relatives or spouses as we grow older. We also seek to soothe ourselves.

Since childhood, most of us have developed preferred methods of self-soothing. For some, it's eating comfort food (or junk food). For others, it's reading a mystery novel, or watching TV. For lots of us, like me, it's both, simultaneously! Many of us run, dance, do yoga, play music. As we become more mindful, we can begin to notice our need for self-soothing, and learn to fulfill it, at least some of the time, in more healthy, or more creative, or even more mindful ways.

If we are currently using unhealthy methods to self-soothe—unhealthy eating, alcohol, drugs, obsessive exercise—acknowledging what we are doing can help us start to minimize those methods. This is especially so if we have begun to cultivate our sense of compassion as part of our mindfulness practice (see chapter 13). The need for soothing (by oneself or others) is generated when we experience pain, either in the present, remembered from the past, or feared in the future. Feeling compassion for the one who is in pain—oneself—is perhaps the healthiest and most mindful form of soothing, and giving it directly to oneself reduces the need to get it from less healthy sources.

Also, by applying mindfulness to a pleasurable activity, whether it is hiking or biking, yoga or dancing or playing the harmonica, we can enhance the enjoyment of the experience while using it as yet another opportunity to build the mental muscle that allows us to be mindful in less pleasing situations.

Desire and Need

Desire is a part of life, and it can be very compelling. Hold your breath for a minute, and you'll notice a very natural and healthy desire—a wanting, a need—for oxygen. It's the same thing with food: don't eat for half a day, and almost anything will taste good. But self-soothing behavior is often accompanied by a particular neediness—almost an addictive quality, although the substances or experiences desired may not be in themselves addictive.

Maybe you always keep the TV on while you're eating. Or you like to eat ice cream before you go to bed. Sure, ice cream tastes good. And maybe it's been a long time since dinner. But something else may be going on, too. Once we become more mindful—more able to look at thoughts as objects in the mind—it's easier to mark the subtle distinctions that identify self-soothing. What's usually present, though probably hidden, is a deep sadness or loneliness or neediness that must be addressed somehow. Ice cream at night is one way to do that, but there may be better ones.

Healthy and Unhealthy Self-Soothing

Some self-soothing behavior is not unhealthy, although it's still useful to be able to identify it. And some behavior that is not intrinsically unhealthy can be used in an unhealthy way. I love to play the blues harmonica. But if I spent every night playing at a bar because I needed the adulation of the audience, that would be an unhealthy usage of a healthy behavior.

Human beings are great at using healthy behavior in unhealthy ways. Dieting can be healthy, but those who are anorectic carry it to an unhealthy extreme. Reading is a great pastime, but doing it to the extent that you have no time to spend with your family is unskillful. I've met people for whom collecting stamps or attending rock concerts has engulfed their lives to the extent that they do virtually nothing else.

Denial, Numbing, and Self-Soothing

Denial might be considered the "evil twin" of mindful dead-end thought diversion. As you may recall, I spent lots of time in chapter 6 discussing the importance of not labeling something a dead end unless you are sure that it is, and being fully aware that a thought that is a dead end in one context may be useful or even important to contemplate in another context. When we divert our attention from a chosen dead-end thought, we do it mindfully, purposefully. In denial, we ignore a thought or situation completely and with no mindfulness at all.

"Numbing," in which we try to immerse ourselves in an activity so as to avoid other aspects of our life, is a type or strategy of denial. It's also easy to confuse with self-soothing, and may indeed be a subcategory of self-soothing. In fact, if our life is painful, numbing can work quite well, or even be skillful at times—like using novocaine during a root canal.

It's noticing and acknowledging what you are doing that's important: "Well, I'm really sick of waiting at the doctor's office,

I've done ten minutes of breathing meditation already and a little compassion work, and I'm going to read the heck out of this *People* magazine." That's a pretty mindful analysis of the situation, in my opinion. Just picking up the magazine as soon as you arrive, and focusing intently on it to avoid your anxiety about the visit? Maybe not quite as skillful.

TV, Talk Radio, and the Internet

Whole books have been published about healthy versus unhealthy use of TV, talk radio, the Internet, and similar techno-pursuits. Here and now, I'll just say what I think about the matter, which is that many people use these technologies as I sometimes do— as a form of numbing. If you use them mindfully—thinking of the pros and cons before you hit the on button, judging when to turn the machine off—they can be entertaining and useful, no better or worse than reading a detective novel. Used excessively, by habit or rote, for numbing purposes, or to avoid mental pain or the work of being mindful, they waste time and, often, because of the exciting, violent, abrasive, and divisive nature of much of the content, they simulate and stimulate un-useful stress responses.

Applying a moment of any meditation before beginning to play that game or check your email or social network page for the fifth time in the hour, then deciding whether it's a good use of your time—this is a wonderful opportunity for building mental muscle, no matter what you decide to do.

What You May Really Be Trying to Accomplish

In my opinion, and in my own life, self-soothing behavior is generally undertaken because one doesn't feel nurtured. Developing a sense of compassion that you can apply to yourself and to others is the truest, deepest way to nurture yourself. If you are a self-soother—and especially if you use self-soothing behaviors that seem less than healthy to you, you may want to read chapter 13, on the subject of compassion, and work with the exercises in it.

The following exercise will give you tools to begin being mindful around your self-soothing behavior.

Exercise 40: Self-Soothing Investigation

1. The next time you find yourself preparing to engage in a possibly self-soothing activity (standing in front of the freezer, spoon in hand, for example), stop for just a moment.

2. Do about a minute of any breath-based meditation exercise.

3. Look for any thoughts or feelings in your mind. Any sadness? Loneliness? Anger? Need for nurture or solace? What's in there right now?

4. Try to do a moment of the self-compassion exercise (exercise 36), especially if you noticed any kind of sad or "needy" feelings (indicating that self-soothing is the goal, rather than the desire for ice cream or the junky novel) in the previous step.

5. Now go ahead and do whatever self-soothing activity you were planning to do.

If you do this repeatedly, you'll eventually become more mindful about this particular self-soothing activity. This does not mean you will cease doing it. But the awareness may help you begin to fulfill some of the needs that underlie the behavior in different ways. This, in turn, can reduce your need for this particular behavior.

A Strategy to Reduce Unhealthy Self-Soothing Behavior

If you would like to reduce unhealthy or un-useful self-soothing behaviors, here are the elements of a strategy to do so.

1. In general, work to develop more compassion. We can never have too much of this. Patience and self-compassion will help you work on your self-soothing issues, especially if you are patient and compassionate while doing so.

2. Identify and name your most commonly used self-soothing behaviors, as you would name any type of thought (see exercise 34, in chapter 12).

3. Honestly assess whether each of the behaviors you've identified is healthy or not. This may vary by context and scale—having a few drinks with dinner on weekends may be fine, but three-cocktail lunches or daily half-pints of vodka perhaps not so good.

4. Apply the self-soothing exercise, above, to these behaviors as you notice yourself doing them.

Combining Mindfulness, Compassion, and Activity to Self-Soothe

Once you have mindfully identified your self-soothing needs and are working on developing your sense of compassion, there are ways you can enhance your healthy self-soothing behaviors—or develop new ones. One good reason to do this is that, often, unhealthy self-soothing activities can create negative self-judgment, even self-hate. However, healthy self-soothing behaviors are just as satisfying, and are likely to enhance positive feelings about yourself.

One of the most important elements of this endeavor will be the "just doing" exercises in chapter 10. If you have not already practiced "just looking" and "just listening," go back to chapter 10 and work on this.

Another important element will be avoiding self-judging, especially if you are learning to do a self-soothing activity that is new to you—like dancing, if you've never danced much. Review the judging exercises in chapter 11 if you have not worked with them much—they will be very applicable to healthy self-soothing activities that are new to you.

Healthy Self-Soothing Activities

Almost any activity that is not unhealthy and has any pleasurable aspect can be used to self-soothe. It doesn't have to be anything very special or glitzy, nor does it have to take very long. It may well be something that you already do without being mindful. Here are some examples.

Baths and Showers and Shampoos

The next time you take a bath or shower, try to do it as a "just washing, just shampooing" exercise. Use a simple breath-based meditation, starting as soon as you get the water temperature right and get into it. No thoughts, no story from the mind, no body judgments. Just breathing, and just bathing. As you soap yourself, try to touch yourself with compassion: "This is my body, my living body, and all living creatures need and deserve compassion." If you notice self-judging thoughts, or any other thoughts, turn your attention back to your breath. Warm water on the body feels good. Enjoy it!

Eating Something Healthy

Wait until you're a little bit hungry, then eat something healthy, something you would not normally consider a "treat" in any way (but not something you dislike). As in the bathing exercise, do a breath-based meditation throughout, so that you can concentrate on "just eating this carrot." Again, if judging thoughts ("I don't like veggies, wish this were a hot dog") or any other self-talk arises, return most of your attention to your breath, split only with the action of chewing and the input from your taste buds. If weight, body image, or eating is an issue for you, you'll need to use lots of compassion and patience with this exercise.

Try a Dancing Meditation

There are a number of meditative dancing practices, but I'm just talking about "regular" dancing. If you don't know how to dance, start by listening to music and simply moving your body to the beat while doing a breathing meditation. If you have a decent sense of rhythm, try coordinating your breath to the timing of the music: four beats to inhale, four to exhale, or three in, three out (since most music is played in rhythms of either three or four beats). Rent or download a "how to dance" video in a style you like, and work with it at home. Again, patience and compassion will help a lot in this endeavor. You may feel confident enough to dance with friends, but just do it in private if you prefer—it's great exercise for the body and the mind.

Try a Shopping Meditation

For many of us, buying things—whether we really need them or not—is a self-soothing practice. The next time you decide to go shopping, use the steps in the strategy to reduce unhealthy self-soothing behavior, above, to investigate whether your shopping behavior is healthy or unhealthy. Perhaps it is sometimes one and sometimes the other. Then when you actually go to the shops, try to practice "just doing" and avoid self-judging while you shop. Try to notice if using these mindfulness tools affects how you shop and what you buy.

For Very Athletic Types

Many athletic pursuits, like bicycling, surfing, or rock-climbing, require intense focus on the mechanics of what you're doing. Serious practitioners of these activities are probably already doing some form of "just biking, just surfing, just rock-climbing"—since they know that distracting thoughts may impair their abilities and a moment of inattention may endanger them. If you are serious about a sport, you may find that the use of visualization can help you improve (see chapter 9). You'll also find that cultivating compassion, though it may reduce your sense of competitiveness, can make your activities more pleasurable.

For Hikers and Joggers

If you hike, or walk, or jog, these exercise forms are custom-made for any of the walking and breathing meditations in this book. You can build mental muscle at the exact same time as you build leg muscle and aerobic capacity. I walk or jog every day while doing either the variable walking meditation with breath-labeling and step-counting (exercise 12: "in…two…three…four, out…two…three") or the simpler walking, breathing, and labeling meditation (exercise 5: "iiinnn…oouuttt").

For Yoga Practitioners

If you do Hatha yoga, try adapting the walking, breathing, and labeling meditation (exercise 5) as you practice. You can try to maintain the breath-labeling throughout your yoga session (this will be easier if you are guided by a teacher or DVD or CD, or if you have a set routine of poses memorized). Or you can begin the breath-labeling once you have placed yourself in each pose. If, like me, you hold certain poses for "a count of ten" or "a count of twenty," you can integrate your "count" with your breath-labeling, so that a count of ten becomes "in…two… three, out…four…five…six, in…seven…eight…nine…ten," or whatever counting scheme fits your breathing. Focus on the "vital breath" or "prana" is of great importance in yoga, so this exercise is completely compatible with any practice. (Naturally,

I've developed a practice called "Prana-Harmonica™," as well as a form of "HarmonicaYoga ™!")

Summing Up

- Self-soothing is a natural part of life, a way of dealing with pain. The better we understand why we do it, the more we can make it a healthy rather than unhealthy practice.

- Many of the exercises you've been learning throughout this book can be used to help you soothe yourself more mindfully. But none is more important than the cultivation of compassion.

- Lots of activities that you already do can be enhanced to make them more self-soothing. Use the suggestions given here to add to the value of what you already do, and try to find your own opportunities to combine your mindfulness practice with your healthy self-soothing activities.

bibliography

References

American Psychological Association Mind/Body Health Public Education Campaign. 2007. *Stress in America Survey.* Washington, D.C.: American Psychological Association.

Csikszentmihalyi, Mihaly. 1990. *Flow: The Psychology of Optimal Experience.* New York: Harper Perennial.

Garfield, Charles A. 1978. *Psychosocial Care of the Dying Patient.* New York: McGraw-Hill.

Resources

Harp, David, and Matthew McKay. 2005. *Neural Path Therapy: How to Change Your Brain's Response to Anger, Fear, Pain, and Desire.* Oakland: New Harbinger Publications.

Harp, David, and Nina Smiley. 2008. *The Three Minute Meditator,* fifth edition. Montpelier, VT: mind's i press.

Kornfield, Jack. 1993. *A Path with Heart.* New York: Random House.

Levine, Stephen. 1997. *A Year to Live: How to Live This Year As If It Were Your Last.* New York: Bell Tower.

Levine, Stephen, and Ondrea Levine. 1982. *Who Dies? An Investigation of Conscious Living and Conscious Dying.* New York: Anchor Press.

Nisargadatta, Sri, and Maurice Frydman. 1973. *I Am That.* Durham, NC: Acorn Press.

Smiley, Nina, and David Harp. 1989. *MetaPhysical Fitness: The Complete Thirty-Day Program for Your Mental, Emotional, and Spiritual Health.* Montpelier, VT: mind's i press.

David Harp, MA, is a corporate speaker, cognitive behavioral therapy trainer, and author of numerous books, including *The Three Minute Meditator*, *Neural Path Therapy*, and *MetaPhysical Fitness*. He specializes in training groups of all sizes and types to consciously control what is commonly known as the fight-or-flight response, which produces fear and anger. Harp is also America's best-known harmonica teacher, with over a million students to his credit. He lives in Middlesex, VT.

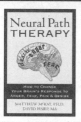